Sphere of Influence

An Approach to Self-Defense

By M. D. Holden
and Rosa Sophia

Foreword by J. Duncan LaPlante

Copyright ©2017 Rosa Sophia
All rights reserved. No part of this publication may be reproduced, stored in a retrieval system, or transmitted in any form or by any means, electronic, mechanical, photocopying, recording, or otherwise, without the prior written permission of the publisher.
Published by Lady June Press
Printed in the United States of America
Library of Congress Control Number: 2017906802
ISBN-13: 978-0-9983773-1-5
First Paperback Edition

For Richie Heller.

"For as the body without the spirit is dead, so faith without works is dead also."

–James 2:26

Contents

Acknowledgments 9
Contributors 13
Foreword 15
Introduction 23
Part 1: Self-Defense and the Sphere of Influence 27
Chapter 1: Correct Context In Training 29
Chapter 2: The Science of Defense 32
Chapter 3: Minimize, Act, Disrupt, Execute 35
Chapter 4: MADE, Grains of Salt 45
Chapter 5: Wing Chun Forms 48
Chapter 6: Fighting the Powell Doctrine 51
Chapter 7: The Targeting System 58
Chapter 8: Sparring Methods 87
Chapter 9: On Facing Your Opponent 92
Chapter 10: A Final Lesson on Your Surroundings 95
Part 2: Knives and the Sphere of Influence 101
Chapter 11: The Modern Knife 103
Chapter 12: Basic Targeting System, Edged Stage 120
Chapter 13: Short Range Knives and Puppet Theory 123
Chapter 14: The Pennsylvania Knife 140
Part 3: Moy Yat Ving Tsun Journal 153
Chapter 15: A Focus on Training 155
Chapter 16: The Holden Group 171
Chapter 17: Final Thoughts 180
Chapter 18: Wing Chun Personal Interview 185

Part 4: Memories and Miles's Personal Sphere of Influence **189**
Chapter 19: Sneak Attack 193
Chapter 20: My Nephew 198
Chapter 21: Childhood Friends 200
Chapter 22: My Son Miles's World Map 202
Chapter 23: Always In Motion 204
Chapter 24: "Why so serious?" 206
Chapter 25: Teacher Meets Student 215
Chapter 26: Letter to Miles 217
Chapter 27: Nǐ hǎo 227
Chapter 28: Memories From Tinicum 232
Chapter 29: The Gift 236
Chapter 30: Expect The Unexpected 239
Chapter 31: Be Prepared 242
Chapter 32: The Helpmate 245
Chapter 33: My Cousin 249
Chapter 34: The Godshall Family 251
Chapter 35: Still Chillin' 254
Miles's Recommended Reading List 264
Glossary 268
Index 272
About M. D. Holden 274
About Rosa Sophia 275

Acknowledgments

This book is a collection of M. D. Holden's writings (Miles Dylan Godshall Holden) compiled by his sister, Rosa Sophia Godshall-Holden. Many thanks are owed to the teachers at Tinicum Art and Science, the private high school we both attended, for encouraging and nurturing Miles's growth in academics and the martial arts. TAS has since closed, and the new school is called the Lotus School of Liberal Arts.

Thank you to Duncan LaPlante and Stephanie Kenney for their unconditional support. Many thanks to Peter Ryan, Chrissy Sinatra, Tina Orphenides, Doug Willing, Matt Kustafik, William Palmieri, Sherry Beers, Roberto Garza, and Buffy Parvin.

My brother noted within this text how much John Heinz inspired him. Thank you, John, for helping Miles to find his passions in life.

Miles's kindness, love, and talent for teaching flourished in part because of Tinicum. Many thanks go to Joëlle Rublee, Matthew Dunar, April Lewis, Christine Bennett, Crystal

Ungaretta, Christie Slingluff, Timothy Ryan Capelle, Julian LaPlante, Ryan Killough and his family, and all of my friends and Miles's friends for being so supportive and helpful during this process. I cannot thank you enough. Many of you helped contribute to this book. A very special thank you goes to April, for sending me Miles's journal, which you can read in Part 3 of this book.

I must also acknowledge the help of my supportive family. Special thanks to Uncle Bob, Grandma Polly, the rest of the Holden family, Gregg Umland and the Umland family, and of course the Godshall clan.

In the wake of our father's loss, there are no words to describe losing my brother, my best friend. We must always remember they are together now—father and son.

There are so many people who played an integral part in Miles's life and growth, that I cannot possibly name them all here. Just know that I am grateful for you, for your help, and for your love.

There was also an entire team of wonderful folks behind the production of this book: Many thanks to you all. Thank you to Laura Kemmerer for her friendship, as well the time she spent proofreading. Thanks must also go to Miles's martial arts teachers, especially his Sifu, Julio Ojeda, who was the first to read the book to ensure its accuracy.

Thank you to Mark Carter for copyediting the book and providing much-needed insight, and thank you to Grand Master Isaiah Gathings of the Academy of Soo Do Thai in Hazel Park, Michigan for his valuable feedback.

Also, many thanks to Scott Patrowich, Bill Koch, and Port St. Lucie Wing Chun for offering classes which have helped me to improve this book, add to it, and make it something my little brother Miles would truly be proud of.

Contributors

The following friends, family, and teachers have contributed to *Part 4: Memories and Miles's Personal Sphere of Influence*. Names are listed in the order their writing or quotation appears.

Rosa Sophia
Brenda Godshall Haberle
Morgan Rank
Ruby Lynn Holden
James Lysoby
Stephanie Kenney
Julio Ojeda
Peter Ryan Sabom Nim
Christine Bennett
Matthew Kustafik
Buffy Parvin
Julia Altabef
Laura Kemmerer

Sphere of Influence

Josh Mertz

Julie Renner

April Lewis

Donna Godshall Hayden

Alyssa Godshall

Ashley Godshall

Nicole M. Castillo

Joëlle Rublee

Foreword

Miles once asked, "Which is preferable, open hand technique or closed fist?"

I replied, "In Goju—a Japanese karate style—they teach almost exclusively closed fist, but at almost every tournament I've witnessed, the open hand technique tends to dominate." Miles considered this for a moment and concluded that it would depend on the nature of the combat and what the intended conclusion would be. Questions—the constant effort to seek knowledge. This, I suspect, is how Miles Dylan Holden built a sense of himself.

Find someone you trust and establish the relationship without fear of conflict, because once the conflict is resolved, the relationship will deepen. This of course, is predicated on the essential component of trust. Question, absorb, be critical, integrate the new information with what you already know to be true. Then analyze, test, observe—a rather complex learning process to be sure, but perhaps this is what we all do since childhood on some level. In Miles's case, it seemed to be a conscious and methodical process practiced and refined over the years. He could spot bullshit and superficial nonsense a mile away. At first this might appear as suspicion or even paranoia, but ultimately I came to view it as his own means of critical thinking and testing theories based on his own life experience.

During the couple of months that Miles lived with me, I was able to observe him closely. He trained diligently every day. He sharpened his blades every day. He sharpened all of my axes and hatchets (never made it to the kitchen knives, which could have used a new edge) and he cleaned his gun, every day. Clearly he believed that if he took care of his weapons, they, if called upon, would take care of him. He also strove to instill this in my son, who while on the Appalachian Trail found this to be true and was thankful.

Miles and I cooked together, dined together, and had wonderful conversations, discussing a myriad of big philosophical ideas. Miles's interests were not limited to the martial arts. For instance, he was an avid student of religion, philosophy, and politics and gravitated to history with alacrity. I may have learned as much from him as he did from me. It seemed to me that his propensity for the humanities rounded out his perspective. He would find the most esoteric books in my library and ask to borrow them. He was an avid reader which certainly broadened his world view. People who read are naturally better writers and those who write consistently are better still.

I've had the good fortune to witness Miles's growth as a writer. He wrote nearly every day—journals, observations, philosophical epiphanies, and analysis of what he'd recently read. Miles once wrote a paper for one of my history classes in which he described the father of Alexander the Great as "a ruthless murdering cross-dresser with a propensity for young boys." Although not stated in particularly scholarly terms, it was evident that he had done rather thorough research and grasped the essence of young Alexander's up-bringing. This was clearly beyond the pale when compared to the other students, most of whom came forth with nothing more than the superficial from Wikipedia. Here was an individual who liked to dig deep, find the origins, phrases, styles, and techniques—enough inquiry to overwhelm almost any instructor. In a way, a teacher's dream.

In Miles's exploration of the martial arts and hand-to-hand, close proximity fighting he, as others have done before him (Bruce Lee comes to mind), realized there is no singular style that supersedes any other. All have their strengths and weaknesses. It's as if one were attempting to create the perfect piano or the best of all possible political systems. Miles realized that one needn't reinvent the wheel, but like science or mathematics, one need only build on those who came before us and refine the wheel.

Thus, his endeavor to create a sustainable style of martial arts that would embrace the best of many international techniques (Brazil, Persia, Arabia, Asia of course, and even Native American), evolved. This synthesis of various styles (even including European fencing) would lead him to focus on close quarters combat techniques. Weapons were certainly not excluded. Although proficient with and knowledgeable about firearms, these were exempt from his thesis. Much like the first soldiers of the civil war who, when ordered to use the newly invented Gatling gun, refused because in their souls, it lacked honor, and didn't give their opponent a fighting chance—like shooting fish in a barrel. There is much to admire about Miles, not the least of which was his manner of discretion (as far as I know, he never betrayed a confidence) and observation. Unlike many, he was capable of under-reacting. His observations and insights were often uncanny and rather astute.

Miles probably would have been a great teacher in any subject for this reason: He had a gift for finding each student's style of learning. I've observed him working with the spectrum from gung-ho bad-asses to those who are shy and lack confidence. He had a clear method and a beautiful kindness. He had a knack, regardless of class size, to work to each student's strengths, not their weaknesses. Miles showed patience without sacrificing discipline. For some, it was simply a matter of the repetition of forms. For others he would permit their minor mistakes to get to the larger sequence. Refinement could come upon mastery of the big picture. For still others, he allowed them victories over himself, which I know he could have blocked without effort, simply to inspire confidence in the student. His body language, his gentleness, and his building of trust were his ultimate strengths.

Not without his faults (who is?), Miles fell into the typical temptations of any young man. He indulged in the usual experimentation with drugs and alcohol which would eventually, so it seems, lead to his undoing. However, his exploration of philosophy and religion were broad, and much like his approach to martial arts, he perceived that nearly all religions shared a hope that the best in the human spirit would prevail with a few generally agreed upon guidelines. This of course seemed like common sense to him and was something a child could ascertain. The burning question for Miles was, why couldn't adults?

After attending one of my classes on comparative religion and reading about the history of religion—not required reading—he naturally questioned what human spirituality was like prior to the axial age, and why we couldn't have a personal relationship with God without the rituals and dogma of organized religion. His natural curiosity led him to church periodically, perhaps for personal comfort in the surrender to a practice, and perhaps for the comfort of having a sense of community with others of a similar mind. Simultaneously, however, with his ongoing spirit of inquiry, Miles read Christopher Hitchens and Richard Dawkins, two of this century's most well-known atheists.

I think everyone involved in the production of this book would agree that it would be Miles's wish that those who read it come away with several things—not only an evolved and sound method for close-quarters combat, but an open mind to new techniques, some of which can be modified to suit one's own body type and size. Further, that humans are not machines and no one is an expert on everything, meaning we should question our teachers (politely, of course) and find the path that is uniquely ours.

We all have the capacity to continuously improve on everything and to continue learning. Reading, experiences, and trusted mentors help this process along immensely. Lastly, I think Miles would like to impart this message: Pay attention. By this, he meant that in spite of our fallibilities we can—and sometimes must—focus our senses on the task at hand. Miles has set forth some methods for this for which he intended us to expand our awareness of our environment and potential threats. It's nearly impossible to care for ourselves or others if we are oblivious to our surroundings.

It's a bit of a cliché for elders such as myself to suggest that such a loss is tragic, but it is nonetheless true. The tragedy is not just in our own suffering for our loss of a dear friend, for the relentless pondering we do as to what might've been. Who might have Miles taught, cared for and inspired to their own, unique path? What might he have been at thirty-five or fifty? What other wisdom might he have acquired along the way?

These, of course, are unanswerable questions we all must live with. I (we) think of him often, have imaginary conversations with him, imagine him with us, and often weep upon doing so. It is, however, uncommon for such a young man, in spite of all the explorations and temptations to which all youth are prone, to maintain a discipline that few possess. He always wrote, he always read, and perhaps the most important to him—he always trained.

– *J. Duncan LaPlante*
Writer and Teacher

Introduction

Sphere of Influence: An Approach to Self-Defense is a collection of writings by M. D. Holden which focus on the art of self-defense. Specifically, this book discusses self-defense techniques Miles practiced daily. It is a book about martial arts, but it is also a tribute to Miles's life.

The book is divided into four parts. Part 1 focuses on the sphere of influence in self-defense. Correct context in training is discussed, the science of self-defense, Miles's brainchild entitled MADE—which stands for Minimize, Act, Disrupt, Execute—facing your opponent, and sparring methods. Any chapter or section that is marked with the sub-heading *Neighborhood Rules* was written while Miles attended Tinicum Art and Science, a private high school. Neighborhood Rules was the title of Miles's senior project, which was required for graduation.

Readers will find that Chapter 5: Wing Chun Forms varies somewhat in style; this is because it is the only chapter that

Miles did not write. I felt that Miles would have wanted the forms of Wing Chun to be explained, so I gathered whatever information I could from his training videos and attempted to write a short chapter about forms without deviating too much from Miles's style. The rest of the book, of course, was written entirely by Miles.

Part 2 discusses the sphere of influence (or SOI) in regard to knives and knife sparring methods. For the purposes of this book, Miles defines the sphere of influence as:

The exact range you can control without moving. In terms of the unarmed combatant: it is the length of your arm. In terms of the armed combatant: it is the length of your weapon. This book is designed to help you gain control over your sphere of influence.

Part 3, the Moy Yat Ving Tsun Journal, is a journal that Miles wrote which follows his training and offers readers an insight into Miles's personal thoughts and ideas about life and martial arts. Readers may notice some repetition in the journal. However, I have decided to keep the journal in its original form in order to preserve Miles's voice.

Part 4 focuses on an entirely different sphere of influence: Miles's own personal sphere of influence. This section examines Miles's life, friendships, goals, and dreams. In Part 4, through the memories and contributions of others, we reveal the influence Miles had on those around him, proving what a full life he led despite his early death.

Miles studied self-defense for over ten years. He took his own life at age twenty-seven. Though we must wonder how much he would have accomplished, had he chosen to live instead, we must also acknowledge how much he did accomplish despite his secret suffering. As a martial artist and certified EMT, Miles was driven to help, to teach, and to learn. Friends remarked how Miles constantly trained in martial arts, and while doing his forms, would talk about the books he had read and the things he learned. Despite all his efforts to help others, and to teach people how to protect themselves, there was one person Miles couldn't protect himself from: himself.

As you read *Sphere of Influence: An Approach to Self-Defense*, know that each passage was penned with passion and dedication. The last time Miles was in my house in Jensen Beach, he sat on the floor in the dining room, his brow furrowed, jotting down notes on martial arts. That is how I have thought of him while assembling this book.

Please remember that this is an incomplete work. Some chapters were written years ago, and some were written recently. The tone of his writing evolved, and the differences are evident in some areas. For example, where MADE is discussed, Miles notes the imperfections in the theory: "But since it is my trail, my mistakes are my own and have to be corrected as I hack away at the dense forest of ignorance—both personal and belonging to others."

Miles didn't profess to be the last word on any topic. His humble attitude shows when encouraging readers to never base their training on just one source, but to continually seek new knowledge: "Think your training through carefully so that you can act quickly when it counts. Always seek a second opinion; doubt even this."

In some cases, I have written a short note in italics at the beginning of a chapter. The note is meant to provide context or explanation in regard to content. Some sections are shorter than others. Readers may discover some areas are lacking something. This is true; if Miles were here today, he would be working on this right now, adding new articles and reassessing old ones. As it stands, we only have what my little brother has left behind. I hope that you, dear readers, feel the passion and motivation that Miles put into his writing, and as an extension, into his work. His own sphere of influence will never be forgotten.

— *Rosa Sophia*

Part 1: Self-Defense and the Sphere of Influence

The bell is never interrupted

Wait one minute,

Five

Or Ten.

The first chime is still there.

— M. D. Holden

Chapter 1: Correct Context In Training

Sphere of Influence: An Approach to Self-Defense was written for a specific target audience: those who already understand some martial arts and have studied self-defense. If a reader intends to study these methods, and apply them to a martial art, it is assumed the reader already has some background on the topics discussed. These methods are meant to protect you against an attacker who intends to harm you physically, but you must already have knowledge in the martial arts.

If you lack background experience in martial arts or self-defense, it is best that you do not apply any of these methods. These procedures are useful, and the ability to protect yourself is valuable. However, the techniques are dangerous if wielded incorrectly.

Read and enjoy, but please—if you intend to employ these techniques, learn and study a martial art first.

This is not legal advice, nor is it a replacement for hands-on instruction, second opinions, and daily training. At its best, this project can plant the seeds of curiosity: Such is the limit of written instruction. There is always room for misinterpretation and improper application. This is of course, your fault—you, the reader—and not mine. Use proper training gear, and crawl before you sprint.

* * *

I am a Wing Chun practitioner, and a martial artist of eleven years. My experience is colored by Korean kickboxing, American Karate, Catch wrestling, and Wing Chun.

Imagine if, in order to become a doctor, one had to learn every facet of medicine—feet, spines, heart surgery, proctology, and more. If you got a splinter and were infected, you would be dead before you could get hold of a certified doctor. The field of medicine is huge, a universe on its own. Violence is much the same.

It begins with tournament fighting vs. reality: rules and regulations, well-lit and courteous against not. Then we can break it down into civilian, military, and police. Each situation has different rules attached to it, not only common sense practice but also parity and use of force.

After that it can be broken down further, how each category differs when the situation changes, weapons or a terrain shift for example. Where a military situation would require escalation, a police response could be totally different—on the books, at least. Much like a doctor—who only studies a manageable amount of fields for the sake of effectiveness—a good combatant shouldn't bog themselves down with an unmanageable amount of contexts that they will never use.

I live in Pennsylvania, but I work in New Jersey. In later chapters, I will also discuss my system of carrying weapons, which was initially thrown into chaos due to my daily commute across state lines. I have carried my knife concealed for eleven years and have sought out much concerning its carry, deployment, and application. I train as a civilian and so long as I am, I will not include a military context. If I were to slip and apply something too harsh, I could wind up in prison. Likewise, I don't include anything too gentle.

Chapter 2: The Science of Defense

First and most important is what you are defending. The most appropriate term I've found is the *centerline*. This line goes from right between your eyes down to the center of your groin. As you defend, also keep in mind the line connecting your centerline to the centerline of your opponent. Imagine the shortest distance between you and your attacker.

The centerline is your most vulnerable area; the issue is how to defend it.

There are three basic ways.

One: Run like hell, and protect your center as it is heading away at a very fast rate.

Two: Attack, and so protect your vitals by ensuring that no severe damage can be done.

Three: Turn your centerline away from your opponent.

Suppose you are facing twelve o'clock. To turn your center *off* line is to turn your torso toward three o'clock. This, however, creates a serious problem: All your weapons are turned away from your opponent. You may defend well, but you can only defend so long before faltering or falling.

A smarter method is to turn to two o'clock. It's a compromise, giving you one-and-a-half weapons and increasing your ability to defend three times over.

The real question is, should you defend at all? Once someone has demonstrated intent to do harm, you should take up a counter offensive tactic. He attacks inside, you attack outside, and if he attacks split, go above or below the weapon.

To do this, you don't need to be concerned about stances so much. You need to remain as mobile as possible. The ability to move in any direction without changing your position is essential to rapid reaction and effective action.

To be counter offensive you must get your hands on his weapons and targets. The philosophy is that the faster you take him out, the less damage he can do. That your vitals are open is secondary in importance. The more you do unto him, the less he can do unto you. The clinch is a scary place to be, but the best way to be in it is if you initiate it. Reaction is always slower and very often, the last thing the loser does is react.

Seeing this, it's ironic that when danger is greatest, the need to turn your vitals away is least advantageous. When you can't attack—in a low intensity struggle—this is the only time that your centerline should be turned away. Where you put your center depends entirely on what level of violence you need to inflict to end the conflict.

If a friend is drunk and getting violent, you can't smash their face in with good conscience, so you're bound to take a few shots before you can ground them and get them into a reasonable mood. In this situation, with so much to defend and no opportunity to attack, it makes good sense to turn your center away.

When a stranger threatens bodily harm, you don't want to risk any more than one shot. Even that one strike could end you if you aren't already committed to neutralizing the threat. If you are committed to defense, but in an offensive stance and are struck, you will be undone because there is too much to defend.

The trick is to always minimize what you have to focus on. If all the targets are open, you need to focus on toppling the threat. If all the targets are closed, it is simplest to focus on defending the few that remain open—as one or two always will be. Minimizing the problems you must deal with minimizes the stress as well as the difficulty.

Chapter 3: Minimize, Act, Disrupt, Execute

MADE (Minimize, Act, Disrupt, Execute) is a series of techniques created by Miles, combined into one approach. The author wrote this portion as a precursor to other writings about this technique. The chapter ends with a note regarding those individuals who inspired Miles in the creation of MADE. It should be noted that this chapter, including the author's note which begins the chapter, was included in an email to friends and colleagues entitled Public Service.

To preserve his voice, I have included the note Miles wrote in the original email.

From: Miles Holden

Date: December 24, 2010 at 2:28:05 AM EST

Subject: Public Service/Sample Piece

Attached is a sample of my basic self-defense blue-print. Please read if you find the time, please send feedback if you find some more [time].

This is my first finished product that I really approve of, though it is no longer a pre-requisite to a weapons course. Now it's just the basic course before 'advanced' combat. I'm sending this en-mass for some feedback, but also because it's generally not a bad thing to do. Enjoy ... or don't.

Miles Holden

Basic Combat Course: Prerequisite to Weapons Course

The means of being a teacher are two-fold. Your information must be easy to remember and has to grow on its own. Basic lessons are a reference point and over time, the students' understanding should expand to include many tactics and situations. Always protect your centerline. The ***centerline*** is the imaginary line running from between the eyes to the genitals and occasionally a leg. Your most sensitive targets are here, excluding the temples, eardrums, and mastoid process.

MADE.

This doesn't mean one thing, it means many things. The breakdown is:

Minimize risk

Act to increase his (your opponent's risk)

Disrupt his ability to continue

Execute your objective

It is designed to teach stance, blocking, attacking,

objectives, and mindset. It has a military context, a civilian context, and even a personal context in relation to how we navigate our lives. There is no limit to how this can be used to enhance your odds of survival.

The first step—regardless of whether we're just getting out of bed, or standing in front of a jacked crackhead—is to *minimize* your risk relative to the variables around you. In combat, it means raising your hands to cover your face and throat. It means bending your knees so they don't get broken and to enhance your speed. It means turning your chin down so your throat isn't exposed.

Its military application could mean buttressing a gate, building defenses or traps, collecting information about your surroundings, or hiring local guides. Its personal application is not eating a pound of junk food, not smoking two packs a day, not drinking yourself stupid constantly.

You're *acting* so you don't have to react. Being proactive is the first tool in your arsenal. When you are limited to response, the odds are always against you. Always move first. For example: There is a huge difference between turning around to find an angry drunk two feet from your face and seeing him from twenty feet away, and stopping him verbally at ten. There is a shockingly large difference between deciding to control the toxins you intake as opposed to a doctor telling you that you are cancerous and have six months to live.

Awareness is the key factor. You must want to deal with life's problems. If you don't want to see danger on your terms, you'll be forced to deal with it on its terms.

Minimizing risk isn't just good tactics. It's common sense.

MADE teaches consequences in its rawest form—blood and bone. It means keeping your eyes open. It means knowing where you are and what is around you. It means having multiple exits and being near cover. It means being aware.

Recapitulation

Our first concern is combat, so let's run through the checklist:

1. Raise your arms to cover your face and throat.
2. Turn your centerline away from the target.
3. Turn your chin down to protect your throat.
4. Bend your knees to increase mobility.

The first is pretty straightforward, but justice can still be done to it. When fighting unarmed, keep your elbows in close. Should his fist make direct contact with them, they could break. As far as defensive fight-enders go, this one is the best.

There are other targets to cover, but the facts don't lie. If he's going to hit you anywhere, it will be the face or throat. Unless you're attacking, the groin is not a practical option. He wants you down quickly, in a way that doesn't disturb the surroundings, and he knows that the best method is to take out the command center.

Typically—despite how aware you try to be—by the time your arms go up, he's already halfway to his target. Considering that his path is probably five feet or fewer, this isn't a surprise. You're probably going to catch the blow and find out afterward as you reestablish distance. The forearms should constantly "patrol" the face, throat, and solar plexus. I call it **Compulsive Cover** and it is absolutely essential.

The second point is more vague—turning *off* line or off-center. When directly facing someone, all your targets are exposed. With one foot in front of the other, the groin is out of the way. As your torso turns to match your legs, the twenty-five percent closed targets turns into fifty percent. With a simple turn, half your targets are sheltered from his first attack. It forces him to either go for your knee or your head. With less to defend, you have less to contend with.

Turning the chin down is only logical, and it's an easy way to differentiate a novice from a professional. If he doesn't bring down his chin, he probably won't cover his face until too late either. He definitely won't know what to do with a kick, and while the kick itself lacks combat efficiency, the punch afterward won't.

Bending the knees is only about mobility in the secondary sense. If you try to kick out a bent knee from a straight angle, it isn't likely to work unless he is in the process of straightening it or if he has the strength of a child. You might injure the tendons, but that won't stop a determined opponent. To damage the knee, the leg must be straight first or assaulted from the side. Since a round kick is extremely easy to counter it becomes a simple matter of always facing the threat.

Another important factor is which direction the balance shifts toward: forward, backward, or in the middle. If your stance drifts toward the rear or holds in the middle, you won't recover from impact effectively. When you're hit, you will instinctively pull back. If you can't shift balance to your rear leg, you will fall. To explain further, you're hit in the face, so you pull back, but too much weight is on the rear leg. So, you can't retreat effectively, and you catch the ground or an object and fall.

If your concern is being kicked in the leg, remember that you must train so that you're able to lift your leg no matter how much weight is on it. It's as simple as learning to jump with one leg. Remember that his primary target won't be your knee in a combat situation. It doesn't disable the target.

* * *

Now that you've done everything you can to keep threats at a safe distance, we can talk about how to deal with them.

Going back to our angry drunk: Let's presume for a moment that he isn't drunk or angry, that he is advancing with intent to do lethal harm. You've tried to stop him verbally, but he just isn't interested.

The first step is minimizing risk. Depending on the exposure—public or private—you'll drop into stance, compulsive cover. What this means in the public sense is that your legs will only be bent to an unnoticeable degree and your arms won't be in a true fighting stance. Your forearms will be up but your palms out toward him. You tell him to stop, and if he doesn't, you will act.

If he strikes, you'll block or parry and assault. If he uses a weapon, you'll parry or distract him and assault. If he is only there to yell, you will deescalate and draw a line in the sand. This has not yet developed into a struggle. You still have a degree of control and you will do all you can to maintain that. Walking into every situation with the intent to fight and win only forces you to make a mistake.

Keep an open mind and act without bringing prior judgment into the situation. This not only stops unneeded bloodshed, it leaves you free to assess his methods. You need to be mentally free to *See, Decide, Act,* **and** *Assess.*

It is not fitting to look at a human as a set of targets to be destroyed outside of a classroom setting. If there are more behind him, it doesn't matter how accurate you are in his destruction. You must be efficient in context. You won't utterly destroy a target; you will *disrupt* his ability to operate to the point that you can complete your objective.

The simplest way to do this—remembering the material covered—is to destroy his balance. Humans are often top heavy or bottom heavy when in a combat stance. If you drive a man back enough with strikes to the face, he will backpedal and fall. If you blow out his knee or sweep him, he'll fall. In the center are all his strongest muscle groups, while toward the extremes are his weakest; by targeting these, you enhance your effectiveness in a way that has nothing to do with his size or training.

We have three objectives: civilian, police, and military. Escape, containment, and termination. To put it another way: public, controllable, and home invasion. To survive without lasting damage, you must apply these objectives. This is the *execute* portion of MADE. Misapplication can result in death, or at the very least, your being maimed.

If you're in unfamiliar terrain, there is no good cause to arrest and question the subject, nor is there good cause to kill him. In unfamiliar territory, fighting unfamiliar opponents, the best option is evasion. Other people could be nearby; they could be with him, with you, or neutral. Either way, you can't calculate their response accurately. Escape, contact the police (you always want to be the first to do so) and know your story.

When your nephew takes some bad acid—a loose example—and loses his head, you can't kill him, nor should you knock him down or run. You detain him, calm him, and question him. The first was a striking context leading to the destruction of his balance. This is the same, but in order to get there, you are using a grappling context. You don't want him bruised: take him down nice and easy, wrap, and arrest.

The final context is reserved for home invasion. Uninvited guests come in and you terminate them with the utmost prejudice. Weapons will be used. At no point do you attempt to control force levels. You are going to destroy his balance, but you are going to do it with a weapon and when he hits the ground, you don't stop. You continue to assault his vitals until you're certain that only a paramedic can revive him.

Remember that your intent isn't to destroy your opponent. It is to complete one of these three objectives. Setting something past your most serious problems is the best way to jump over, or totally neutralize them.

Don't think of your enemy, think of your future. You have things to do, a life to live.

Don't let him be the meaning and the end of it.

Get past yourself, get past your target, and get to your objective.

Credit Owed

Destruction of Balance: Carl Cestari

See, Decide, Attack, and Assess: Blaise Loong

Inspiration: John Heinz, and Larry Wic

Chapter 4: MADE, Grains of Salt

Miles wrote this portion as a follow-up to the previous article (Chapter 3) which describes techniques of self-defense in relation to MADE. Where Miles mentions the e-mail entitled Public Service, and the attachment titled MADE, he is referring to the document that makes up Chapter 3.

Here, he discusses flaws he discovered in his creation of MADE, yet continues to point out the importance of these techniques, and how the approach can be examined further based on how it relates to particular situations.

As he notes, the system works well as a concept, yet "when applied to reality it's much different." Nevertheless, MADE offers students of self-defense something important to consider, a useful set of techniques, a solid theory that can truly benefit the martial artist.

* * *

MADE is definitely my brainchild and the cup which holds my pride and the knowledge that I'm not just following someone else's trail. But since it's my trail, my mistakes are my own and must be corrected as I hack away at the dense forest of ignorance—both personal and belonging to others.

There isn't anything wrong with the idea, just the way it was originally conveyed in the e-mail titled Public Service and the attachment titled MADE. Too rigid and mathematical. Too static. Combat is dynamic and fluid. While tips and guidelines help, they can hurt if they are phrased as commandments.

The system works well when looked at from a conceptual viewpoint, but when applied to reality it's much different. For example, a stranger follows for too long, and so you stop them. You minimize your risk by acting first—M and A out of the way—but it's highly unlikely you'll have to disrupt anything. All you need to do is leave. That's M, A, and E—but not really D. We can ponder what really constitutes Disruption, but that isn't nearly as profitable as simply training to accommodate the possible holes.

If someone attacks immediately, and you can't get your hands up or get a word in edgewise, you immediately move into violent disruption—grabbing, twisting, punching, and tearing anything vital in order to protect yourself.

In the beginning, this system should be taught rigidly. Physical or verbal minimization should be followed by action, effective disruption and the completion of the objective. Once it's understood, though, the whole thing needs to fall apart. If it doesn't, you run the risk of retreating when it's time to advance and defending when it's time to attack.

This will leave you, at the very least, maimed.

All systems are castles made of sand, and must be taken with a grain of salt.

Chapter 5: Wing Chun Forms

Since Wing Chun is my main focus and the art form I currently practice and teach, I want to provide a basic background on forms. These are the three main sets of hand forms used in Wing Chun:

Siu Nim Tau

In the first set of forms, horse stance is taught and the legs are strengthened. Directing energy through the movements is important, and this is part of what is learned in Siu Nim Tau. This is the foundation of Wing Chun. It is important to move slowly and pay close attention to each detail of the form.

Cham Kiu

This is the second set of forms in which students learn kicking techniques, creating power in striking. In Cham Kiu, we learn footwork, how to properly shift your weight, timing, and more.

Biu Ji

This is the final set of forms that teaches emergency

approaches that will help during an attack, or if the attacker pins you down. In Bui Ji, we also learn elbow strikes.

Because the art is roughly three hundred years old, it has undergone many changes. Different martial artists have different approaches to the form. I study the Moy Yat lineage of Wing Chun, and each lineage has its differences. The forms discussed and mentioned here are: Siu Nim Tau, Cham Kiu, and Biu Ji. I will also discuss techniques such as Pak Sau, Fook Sau, Tan Sau, and others. To properly understand what is being discussed in order to apply it, you must study and learn Wing Chun. I approach my art from a perspective of continuous learning, keeping in mind elements of the previous art forms I've studied—namely Shim Gum Do.

I've already discussed the centerline and protecting vitals. While it's important to be vigilant, you also want to remain relaxed within your structure. For example, when you move from defense to attack and fight back against your attacker, the energy of the attack should move out at the last possible moment. A good example of this is the way a proper punch should "snap" at the end, releasing energy toward the opponent. One of the things we learn from the forms is how to direct energy. As you continue to practice Wing Chun, you will become more familiar with when it is best to be relaxed, and when it is best to mimic a wrecking ball to protect yourself against your attacker.

Each form provides you with the tools needed to be prepared to protect yourself. I have also worked on applying Wing Chun forms to edged weapons, using the concept of Pak Sau to Pak with both the hand and the knife alternatively. Before you bring a weapon into your Wing Chun training, you must be familiar with all the forms. If you haven't already, find a qualified instructor or school and dedicate yourself to study.

Chapter 6: Fighting the Powell Doctrine

This chapter was previously published as an article on the Blade Ops Blog on January 27, 2015.

Some things are invented, most things are discovered. The tactics of modern battlefields always predate that battlefield; in the mind of the successful attacker rests some degree of the dynamics of educated combatants. If one thing can be assumed, it's that anyone who believes they are dangerous to you *is* dangerous to you and there must be a reason why.

There are many tactics and tools that one could assume the enemy has. A person could become bogged down trying to understand what is common and what is rare. Understanding certain overarching laws can save you that trouble and keep you in class and in the gym, sharpening your skills instead of getting lost in rabbit holes.

In essence, the ***Powell Doctrine***—named for General Powell—is an attitude that tactics and tools are filtered through. It's the philosophy of hitting as hard as you can, as early as you can. Surprise is its primary asset, like hearing the whip and only having that data to react to; in such a case, you are already struck.

This piece won't be long, but I am hopeful that it will be long enough to show you how you can maybe see that whip and the man holding it before its deployment. This will be a treatise on thinking, not action. For those who think they can survive without study, may this show you how wrong you are.

Sphere of Influence, Trinity of Force: Numbers, Weapons, and Power

Robbery, rape, and murder are all confidence games. What I mean by this is that *without* confidence, these crimes wouldn't occur. The violator must believe they are superior. This exists on a sliding scale but it's universal.

The 9/11 hijackings are an example of this. Sure, they're only coming with box cutters, but you say "only" because you may have a shotgun in your closet or a four-inch knife on your person. With only empty hands to offer, a box cutter is a severe life threat. If you aren't aware of these factors, you will become your enemy's "slam dunk" and life will never be the same.

Tackling the issues in order, it's a serious risk to engage one target by yourself. Should you find yourself against a lone combatant, be skeptical of your eyes; odds are good that wherever your weak point is, another combatant is waiting for you there. We don't point rearward. The only thing that can strike backward with any effect are the elbows and it will not be a fight ender if you can't face and engage that threat immediately after.

A solution that doesn't involve hyper awareness or eyes in the back of your head is to exit behind your opponent. If someone is attempting to box you in, you neutralize them and circle toward their back. Not only is your safest exit behind them, so is the safest point to engage from. It's also an opportunity to use your first opponent as a human shield, if needed.

Weapons are an issue so serious that martial artists who consider themselves competent will seek knowledge and training in these tools, knowing that at some point the enemy's weapon—whatever it may be—could enhance them well beyond the skills of any unarmed combatant.

I've heard odd numbers now and again. The idea that comes to mind first is that a martial artist of a year takes on the ability of an artist of five or more years just by picking up a knife. Attaching any number is silly, but the point is hard to miss: Weapons increase lethality. All the man needs is luck after that and you will become past tense.

Taking on weapons is always ill-advised if you came to the party empty handed, but you must do what is easiest even if it's terrifying. When confronted with fight or flight conditions, you must be able to discern which option is safest and easiest. Assuming you engage, there is little I can impart to you from here, save to remind you to cover your head and neck first and engage viciously. Leave your opponent on the ground and unable to follow as you escape.

Concerning how you engage as an armed citizen, remember that it isn't your job to match his weapon, but to exceed it. Fair fights are butchery. You may be incredibly well-versed with your stick or knife, but all they have to do is want victory more.

Finally, we come to power, which is part illusion, part reality. Muscle and size aren't a power, but they are a layer that will interfere with power transfer in striking as well as your ability to kick effectively or defend. When someone like that has the mount on you, the only thing that's going to save you is a weapon or a friend. When someone thinks they can kill you singlehandedly, don't challenge them on it. Keep your weapons and friends close because no man can kill many while unarmed, and none can fight effectively with half a magazine of bullets in them.

Protecting the Sphere of Influence: Drawing a Line in the Sand

In combat, we need space to live. Actually, we need space to *think*. We need time to respond effectively and that requires space. If you reach your hand out, you are touching the limits of your ***Sphere of Influence***. This is the space which someone must penetrate in order to negate all of your skill and ability. You can stop one thing at that distance, but only something you've stopped a million times before, something you've trained for.

Thinking you can prevail at this range is half a fallacy. It's only half because it may well be true; it becomes a full-fledged fallacy if you actually put yourself in that position. The space you want is several miles. The space you may have to settle for is one full step away from your sphere of influence. This is traditionally thought of as the minimum measurement of the ***Line in the Sand***.

It's just enough time for the brain to say "incoming" and for the body to respond effectively. The Tooler Drill paints an even graver picture, showing that a person can close from twenty feet before a pistol can be produced and actuated. You train to be comfortable up close, but don't ever think that means you should be.

Know the Ground: Tricks, Traps, and Exits

In many fights, the ground is as great a threat as the person you face. When you fall, it never misses. When ignored, it takes on the intention of whomever is paying attention to it and can use it. A fire hydrant is stronger than any sidekick, a bench is a takedown that can't be countered, and a wall is the one way to punch someone everywhere all at once.

Gentle grades in a sidewalk will disrupt balance. A fighter will seldom lift their feet to advance and even more seldom while moving backward. Carl Cestari was an advocate of only stomping when moving. The moving Jong of Wing Chun was something I initially distrusted on that account. The truth is that you must fight two battles—one with a human, the other with the ground. Both must be watched and both demand different approaches.

As for exits, there are two kinds: exits in known areas and exits in unknown areas. In familiar terrain, you have choices. You can be through the door immediately. In unfamiliar terrain, there is only one safe exit. Once the engagement has begun and you can no longer look around, it is behind your opponent.

Properly Equipped: The Law, Friends, and Planning

Everything done well requires forethought. If I'm unsure

about a thing, I will bring a friend or two—preferably someone who has already been where I'm about to go. It changes your unknowns into *knowns* all of a sudden. In this way, humans can be even more valuable than weapons, though the presence of friends doesn't invalidate weapons. The ability to avoid a fight—to practice discernment—is by far the best way to carry.

I carry the Heckler & Koch Plan D knife, tucked into my wallet on my strong side. It's shaped like a Kabar TDI, but with a thinner, more useful profile. It can be drawn like a gun and the angle is nearly identical. Its location on my body also allows me to skip a step in production. I no longer have to clear my cover garment as the pocket itself serves to conceal the weapon.

In this instance, I have managed to carry while still being in harmony with the police jurisdictions I pass through en route to and from work. I've had to sacrifice, but I still run efficiently. There are situations where I'll pay a little more to avoid "unfree" areas, but when it can't be avoided, I will adjust. Thinking flexibly, being proactive, and staying optimistic are sometimes your only assets. Never leave them at home.

Chapter 7: The Targeting System

Neighborhood Rules

The full targeting system is taught in three stages—boxing, knife techniques, and stick fighting. *(The knife techniques of the targeting system will be discussed in Part 2.)* This is a medium range system, which means that it places you about three feet from the target. I don't focus on tournament style fighting or dueling. Every real world encounter will be sudden and close up. There will be no bows or squaring off, no complex technique or retreating. You must be quick, proactive, simple, and brutally effective. Nothing complex can be made effective in combat.

The primary focus of this piece is boxing and knife fighting. Stick fighting is more of a long-term side project. Though stick fighting is important, a stick falls in the category of a foreign weapon or a weapon found during combat. Though it's the end result to be proficient with foreign weapons, it is not central to this writing. This is about applying your fists. It is also about applying the knife, a weapon and tool that no one should be without as we cannot simulate its effect with our bodies. *(More discussions regarding the knife as a tool will follow in Part 2 of this book).*

In the boxing stage, the first lesson is how to punch. It seems simple but it isn't. The fine details in even a jab make the difference between a slight poke and a brutal front punch. The student must begin hardening their hands immediately. Because of the nature of real combat, it's even more important than blocking. Blocking and cover are taught afterward. The difference is fairly simple. Blocking implies retreating. Even though you are moving the attack out of the way, you're still just defending and you will be attacked again if you don't retreat. Cover is a technique used during an advance; you are attacking and your other hand is the shield. It isn't a rope-a-dope method as this system depends upon never sitting around during a fight. It is simply a method of covering the primary vitals that would otherwise be open during the shift of defense.

The next stage is combinations and footwork. Tactics are taught within that, but the primary point is fluidity and power in technique. The key is what to punch and what not to punch, and how to make the opponent hit targets that are too hard for their fists.

The footwork is mostly evasive in nature, but not in the sense of a retreat. You get out of the way without creating a gap between you and the target. Remove yourself from harm, but not danger; this way, you can strike the target but not be stuck.

The footwork is molded under the dangers of terrain and gross motor skills. Nothing is too complicated or unrealistic.

Overview of Boxing Stage

1. Punching and the Stance
    - a.) Setting the weight into the strike
    - b.) Turning the shoulders and body into the strike
    - c.) Exploding into the target
    - d.) Hardening the knuckles and hands
2. Counter offensive Technique
    - a.) Cover tactics
    - b.) Footwork and combinations
3. Tactics
    - a.) Escalation
    - b.) Sucker punch
    - c.) Countering kicking technique

In this writing, the boxing stage is broken down differently. However, it is still the same formula. This is just simpler. The formula in the writing explains this, starting with the approach. The one above begins with the assumption that you already understand the approach. Basically, the approach is long and mid-range combat—blocking, kicking, and retreating.

The above formula starts at the point right before close quarter combat, hence making blocking much less necessary. Most fights start there; that's the only moment you must win, and if you waste time blocking, you'll be screwed. Hit him now or it's all over; there will be no need to block.

The last section of the approach is called taking the first strike, and it's at that point that defense is thrown out the window and the targeting system becomes what it is. Blocking has a place, but in a street fight your one and only intent is to attack. You need technique that fits that perfectly. Blocking is replaced by cover, and the drive to destroy replaces the drive to protect the self. This is how to win as the moment is fast and slippery; if you don't jump on it right away, it will hurt or kill you. This doesn't mean always destroy; be decisive and do things as though you fully intended to do only that.

Unarmed Combat

Never leave home without your weapons because you never know exactly what stalks you or what might attack you. Though this starts as an unarmed system, it is made in a world where unarmed is merely an appearance, an assumption that isn't worth dying for. Combat has no limitation. There will be no show of hands or boundary lines. Men will become animals and society will be lost. We must not bring the assumption of society into a place where concepts can't harden. We must be utterly realistic and everything, including our personal feelings, must be thrown to the side as though they weren't ours. There's a great chemical change in the body but chemicals do not equal emotion.

Your body is pumped full of adrenaline and you're taken to a place where action becomes one with thought. If you're afraid, you will act afraid; if you're angry, you will act angry. No one can hide their colors in a fight. If you forget your colors and only concentrate on the moment, though, you will be fighting clearly. Instead of reacting to your own thoughts and fears, you should react to the opponent and the environment because that is the only true threat.

The way I have structured this system is in three stages—explosion, follow-up, and finishing technique. The explosion is the change from a relaxed situation to a fight. It is imperative that you strike first or you will find yourself on the other side of this progression. The moment that the explosion happens, you must strike. We all know what deep shit smells like, and the moment it hits the air we should already have made our decisions.

You must find a suitable opening and explode on it. From there you move to the follow-up stage. This is the battering section of the fight; your intent is to beat the opponent until they choke out. The more openings you tag, the more you will have to target. His guard will drop until he hits the ground and if you persist, there's no way to fail. Finishing techniques include chokes, locks, and submission moves. Chokes and take-downs are the focus, however.

This system is designed for ambush situations wherein the target pops up and now is the only moment left. You must go from where you are; a combat stance will prepare the enemy for combat. You must be in his face without cocking the fist, without using typical footwork. Then, you can either run and possibly get shot, or completely freight-train the target and make sure you walk away. Functional survival does not live up to the ideals of society or government, but neither of the two can live in such a setting anyway. Abandon all you bring, or drown under the weight.

* * *

Your *approach* is where you stand at the moment, and from which direction you advance on the enemy. You must always switch to a new set of targets and stay on the weak side of the opponent. Should you attack a well-defended target, you will be countered and wrecked. Your approach has to be sound and logical. It can rely on objective fact alone. When you don't have an edge on hand, you must depend more upon the core and head as targets. Depending on how the opponent's arm is placed, targets will open and close, shifting your approach.

It isn't the open targets that you should focus upon, and it is useless to concentrate on closed targets. You must see and understand the shifting of the two. When the arm covers the head, almost the entire torso is open, but everything except for the floating ribs can be closed off quickly if the enemy drops the upper arm down. These slight shifts can change the odds in a fight. If you cannot perceive these shifts accurately, you'll never win.

Breaking habit is central to solidifying your approach. Creating new habits can confuse opponents to the point that they can't move out of the way. The habit can be a shift from fear into madness, anger to fear. It just has to make the target advance under false premises. Understanding your own habits comes from a mix of contemplation, training, and experience. All these things are is a questioning mind, however, a complex result that comes from a simple choice.

If you can't break a habit, the next option is to just mask it. In combat, it can be a man who acts afraid until the opponent has left a vital target open but it can be applied to anything, anywhere. Put simply, you have to look past the players to the cards they're holding. You must play the game without considering the risk, and from there learn the best strategy to win. Don't get distracted by sly faces or a hard exterior. Thinking of your own well-being isn't a good thing to see a fight through; you have to see the target and the path between the two of you, and you have to forget about other option because, by now, they have all been tried.

An opening must be acted upon in combat. It appears and we must react properly to it. Waiting for another one is idiotic. There is only that opening, and you must act on what you know, not on what might be. You have to concentrate on ***damaging the target*** rather than protecting yourself. If you attack quickly and solidly enough, there will be much less opportunity to counter and you will wind up with much less damage than with a defensive mindset. The longer you wait, the more the opponent can observe your style, and this is lethal. It prolongs the fight and creates an emotional and mental exchange between the fighters, a sort of mini-relationship. Ideally, you don't look on the opponent as a human but as a target. You don't want to be in any position to understand what it's like in his shoes. ***Targeting*** distracts the mind from emotions. The opponent is considered instead of the self, but the opponent is just a set of targets being watched.

Removing emotional content helps angry people control their temper and weak people to control their fear. The objective becomes all-important and there is no distraction. The result is a cold, quick, super efficient fight. Targeting extends past distraction because you are focusing on the information required to win. You aren't being distracted from anything valuable; you are being distracted by what you need to survive.

Watch for openings, weak points, movement and the shift of defense. Not only must you recognize these things in the moment, but you have to be able to accurately predict how they will be in the next moment. In real life, we can't get that background information, and it's a damn shame. There isn't enough time and we have to act on information that amounts to a grain of sand in comparison to what you want. You'll act in the same way, however, you just won't have as much time to consider the information.

Trust in your process, and train diligently so that it works when there is no time for a system check. Without genuine faith and confidence, you are riding entirely on luck; you have no way of knowing if your method will crumble and have no way of adapting afterward. All of your decisions must be made beforehand.

* * *

The core of *first strike strategy* was summed up for me as: "Be professional, be polite, but have a plan to kill everyone you meet." You must be able to go from relaxed to tense in less than a second; the strike must be the first clue of any aggression. This means that you must already have an attack planned. You must know the fight before it exists and you have to feel nothing for it. The beauty of it is that they have no time to prepare; they cannot resist the strike in any effective way, creating a sort of pure damage. In an ambush, this ability is key.

When you are rushed, there's no time to prepare or even consider your situation. You must simply act. If you don't practice, you may not deliver a powerful strike. You may be too easy to read and get hit before you even steal the first strike. Without complete faith in yourself, you will stumble worse than someone without the physical ability. Winners walk into the fight knowing it's already over. They have made their decision and will follow through at any cost.

The first strike strategy is the key to self-defense, if such a key even exists. Waiting until an attack comes is not in your best interest. If there's a threat and the threat has chosen you, then war must be declared on every level. Legalities are not an issue between you and a crackhead, or you and a mugger.

They won't sue, and you won't be mugged—happy ending.

If you don't even let them make the opening threat, you will become the attacker. There are many levels to this application, however, it can be applied verbally, through body language or physicality. As always, your situation dictates the use. This is why clarity of mind is key. Always make sure you can adjust to your situation. In order to apply the first strike strategy, you must hide any intent to do harm. You must go from relaxed to tense during the strike, not before. There can be no setup. There can be no cocking of the arm because that tells the opponent that the fight has begun. You have to start the fight and make contact simultaneously.

Four Factors of Combat

The idea of the follow-up strike is that you don't just hit the target and run for your life, you attack the target and make sure he can't run at all. After your first strike, the target is stunned. If you keep into him, you may possibly decimate him without taking damage. Ideally, you knock him until a stun sets in. Every opening is tagged until he's either senseless enough to choke out or throw down. Like everything else, the fighting part of combat is short compared to all the other elements. Still, this is everything you train for: conditioning, training, and consistency to survive in the most primitive form of combat. Street fighting, however, adds other methods to the mess.

The first factor in combat is the ***environment***. Having the high ground or the downhill charge, having weapons or using outside units against the target via human shields or good old-fashioned ducking. Coaxing others to fight or hurling the primary target into secondary targets are other methods. Of course, in the updated version, it's just bashing an attacker's head into a brick wall or stomping someone into the street, which is somewhat similar to the original methods. These facts are better accepted than rejected because concrete is a real environmental threat that you must keep on your side.

The second factor is ***weaponry***, on you and in the environment. You should never be without a weapon. There are times when you won't be able to 'compete' without one, and having a weapon you are familiar with makes all the difference. Nearly all weapon techniques are applicable to a stick, and there are sticks everywhere—pool cues, chair legs, collapsible batons, copper piping, table legs, and so on. A standing vacuum cleaner is an excellent weapon if the weight is properly applied. So is a candleholder. There isn't one thing on this planet that can't become a weapon.

The third factor is the target itself—***the opponent***. You shouldn't see a man, you should see movement, openings, targets, and the shift of defense, but never a man, not even if it talks.

And finally, though less important, the forth factor is ***the self***. It must be watched carefully to make sure that the face and body language does not betray the mind. Should you need to deceive the target, you have a plan, and it must be protected, particularly from the self. All of these things must be watched intently.

Covering Head and Neck

The closer you get to the opponent, the less likely blocking gets. ***Cover*** is about the same except you aren't attempting to parry the attacks, just shield yourself from them. There is no perfect way to protect yourself. You will be hit, and most likely, very hard. Remember that it's all about making the opponent fail, not winning. Ending it quickly is your primary interest, and that's why you're so close to the opponent.

The main target to cover is the head and neck. Should you take heavy strikes to the carotid artery, spine, or skull, you'll be on your ass. Conditioning can raise your endurance in the torso, and skull shots hurt less over time, but the less you get hit, the better. Remember that every shot you block or cover is an opening that is limited but valuable. A block must be an attack. Staying on the weak side of the opponent is also a form of cover, but if weapons aren't involved and your opponent has two arms, they may not have a weak side. If you heavily damage one knee, you can create a weak side.

Make him go where he can't follow, and let the environment take a chunk out of him. Always try to break or seriously damage a limb so you can have a weak side to rest at, should the fight go on so long. In a situation with multiple opponents, it's a good idea to apply human shields. Nearly tagging their own people should create a slight stun, and because they have to back off, they create an opening. Don't just see one or two scenarios; consider it as a concept and apply it to random scenarios. Everything can be cover.

Chokes and Finishing Technique

You don't want any problems with the "dead" waking and sneaking up on you after the fight ends. You must know they won't be a threat to you for fifteen or twenty seconds. Knocking someone out can take a while and does a lot of physical damage that makes you look bad in court. Choking them out properly takes about seven to thirteen seconds and you can actually feel them passing out. You know they won't be a problem. The proper application of a choke requires the arms, shoulders, and torso, with a squeezing energy like a snake rather than a choking energy like an arm. Choking someone like a snake is much more effective because even though it tightens at a slower rate, it's stronger on nearly every level and can continue tightening for a long time after a typical choke would reach its peak.

The slow choke creates panic and impairs the judgment of the opponent. Mix this with the physical damage caused by the choke, and the likelihood of escape or counter is drastically reduced. On the mental level, every time he adjusts to the technique, it tightens and he must readjust. Because you are only working toward one thing and he is working toward several, he'll choke out before a reversal or escape is possible. When you slap in with full force, you only give the opponent one situation to deal with. You have gone the limit and he has only one thing to adjust to. You should confuse his mind with a flurry of attacks, even if it's the same attack.

Remember that a choke isn't a limited technique. It is a concept that can be applied differently depending on the situation. If it better served you, it could be applied with the legs or the entire body. It's only a matter of figuring out how to apply pressure and where. You're still only going after targets, targets that change and shift easily. I know I'm not the first to say it, but don't be technically bound. Most chokes concentrate on the carotid arteries and the windpipe. That's all you have to do. Get good pressure on these targets and squeeze. It can be done with anything, from body parts to belts. Look for these kinds of tools in combat because efficiency is the key to survival.

Cross Choke

The best way to execute a front choke is to pin the arms and mount the body so that the legs are too far away to counter you. Pinch the elbows down with your knees and do not let the target wriggle away. Push down into his elbows and don't let up. Techniques can also be shifted to crush the windpipe and this concept might be ideal in reality but you must remember to clear the scene after it's over. Try to damage him severely but try not to kill him.

A cross choke puts pressure on the carotid artery or the windpipe, but if you want to put pressure on both, it won't be completely even, though still effective. The typical cross choke is done when the opponent lands on their back and you mount the chest. The forearms are crossed above the wrist but below the elbow. Each hand is planted on the ground at either side of the neck, just barely touching. The cross in your arms provides the pressure. To increase pressure on the carotid arteries, squeeze the elbows together. To put pressure the windpipe, push down where your arms cross.

This technique derives from Brazilian Jiu-Jitsu, but because our focus is concrete fighting, I don't go beyond the mounted position. If you must roll on concrete, then that's just what has to be done. You should train to that end as well, but this system is all about avoiding that by decimating the target quickly enough so that he never gets his hands on you.

Still, a choke is a great end to a fight. It is assurance of an escape and though front chokes aren't foolproof, they are functional—very functional if the drowning strategy is applied. There's also a more effective method that is far easier to execute and takes down the target in half the time. The above technique is only mentioned because this choke is a lever choke, and without the lever it couldn't be applied. You mount the target in the same way, but you grip the collar of his shirt and pull. The elbows go inward instead of outward, and the pressure, due to the shirt, is magnified. The windpipe still stays relatively unharmed. This method takes far less practice and is ideal in the "heat of the moment."

Lever / Street Choke

A lever choke is a choke applied with the use of an outside tool like a garrote or belt. The street choke is a lever choke, but it doesn't use an outside tool. Instead, it is dependent on the opponent's t-shirt. The beauty of this technique is apparent in the completely even pressure around the neck.

The downfall of it is lousy manufacturing.

On the chance that they have a well-made shirt on, it's good to train with this technique. It's done by grabbing both shoulders and getting a firm grip on the collar of the shirt. One hand is taken around the back of the opponent's head and pulled tight at the other side of the neck after it crosses the other hand. It is wise to move behind the opponent when you have this locked in. There's no safe place to be when you are right in front of the opponent with your hands distracted and his hands free.

Blood Choke / Rear Naked Choke

This is the highly effective seven second choke method. Once this is locked in, they aren't going anywhere. There are methods of stopping it from choking you, but no truly effective means of escaping or reversing the fully locked-in technique. The design of the inner arm fits perfectly against the windpipe and carotid arteries. The pressure is even and incredibly powerful. The angle of approach is from behind the opponent. In combat, this can be hard to create, but it is not impossible.

A choke slap is a fine way to begin this technique. It stuns the opponent long enough for you to drag him off his feet and fully lock in the choke. To perform the choke slap in this instance, the inner forearm is the striking area. You approach from behind and whip your arm around, slapping into the windpipe. After you have made contact, you squeeze in with your arm so that the inside of your elbow is against the windpipe. Bring your other arm up so that the elbow is on the level with your choking hand, grip the choke hand with the inside elbow, and squeeze the hand with your arm. Next, take your free hand and slide it behind the opponent's head as if your hand were a two-by-four or bar moving in front of a door to keep it closed. Then, slide the choking arm (the arm across the opponent's neck) back by rolling your shoulder and sliding it back toward you.

The key to this is maintaining a powerful choke. Your choke arm should harden, flexing as much as possible into the targeted windpipe and arteries. Pull back your shoulders and inhale as much as possible. Try to puff up your entire torso.

Drowning Strategy

If you aren't in the position to execute an effective choke, the drowning effect can immobilize them long enough to get in a better position. Repeated strikes to the arteries and solar plexus stun the target to the point where a choke can be easily applied. Artery pinching is about the same in effect. It requires a bit more skill but can be effective against the carotid artery because of the lack of protection in the neck.

The drowning strategy can also cut down on the choke time or the chance for resistance when dealing with a larger, stronger target. Sometimes this tactic can be lethal. Repeated strikes to the "wind" targets can cause a heart attack but this is extremely rare. A collapsed ribcage is much more likely. All you know is that you have to put everything you've got into it. When someone is trying to cause extreme damage to you, they are unlikely to give in and there's no limitation on possible situations. Better to be the death dealer than the death receiver.

Blunt Targets – Eyes

Striking the eyes is the oldest trick in the book and can be done any way you please and still create damage. Any contact with the eyes will make them water and close. Even if you don't hit them, he'll still blink and step back. Sand is even better, though rare in terrain these days. Mace doubles for it well, but reactions to mace are varied enough that it can be an unreliable option.

The most important part of these targets is your ability to apply the concept more than your fist. If the target is particularly well-defended or well-built, find an enhancer or lever. Grabbing the face has about the same effect. You're trying to take away sight, not just damage the eyes. It all comes down to controlling the senses to distort reality long enough to effectively finish the target.

Eardrum

The hand is kept relaxed but not dead. When it hits the eardrum, it creates a vacuum, and even if they don't go deaf they'll be in serious pain. This would be a bitch slap were it not so well-placed. This is a high-damage area to exploit, so abuse it with care. The fingers are relaxed but the thumb is sticking to the palm. The striking area is solid but everything else is relaxed. The target is dead center of the ear. The striking area is dead center of the palm. Sometimes it's good to anchor the head by grabbing the hair. If the opponent panics, they'll take their arms to the other side of their head, leaving the eardrum exposed.

If your opponent is skilled and attempts this maneuver on you, a good counter for this technique is the eye jab or half-fist to the throat. You need to disrupt their system to the point that they release their grip, like if you were to punch them in the face. When someone grabs your hair or neck, go for what really counts and you will be able to force them to retreat. If you try to undo it with brute force, you'll find yourself missing a chunk of hair—or worse.

Temples

This is an excellent target for controlling and distracting the senses. Striking here creates a small delay in which the opponent is blind and staggering. When dealing with larger, heavier targets, it's best to come in on the temples with both hands, clapping like cymbals but holding steady like a vice. The hammer fist can be applied, but you'll lose a lot of speed, and though powerful, it is too easy to counter or escape. After a temple strike, it is possible to lock in a choke or throw the target before they regain awareness. Power strikes are best if you don't want to get involved with the target for one reason or another. The target area is located just a centimeter past the limit of your peripheral vision and continues for an inch and a half toward the back of the skull.

Countering this is simple, should your opponent be skilled enough to attempt the move on you. Just move your arms out to block both strikes and check your targets. You could go for something classic and throttle him, or you could dig your thumbs into his eyes and toss him on the ground. The best method is to grab their chin and the back of the head. Twist it up in one direction and go full circle and down toward the ground in the other direction. You won't be able to break the neck, but you will create serious pressure. It's too much crank to resist and they will hit the ground.

Solar Plexus

No one can say how effective this is with a hand technique but multiple blows creates the drowning effect. Matched with a solid choke, your problems will be over quick. The target is the opening in the ribs at the bottom of the chest. Striking here will wind the target. Multiple strikes could collapse the ribcage. The best method is an uppercut into the ribs with a ripping force up toward the heart. Direct blows to the heart do nothing as the ribcage protects us from that.

Drowning can be simply defined as being without air. There are many ways to create this effect, and the above tactic stops the intake of oxygen by timed, blunt bursts. Other techniques include filling a space with liquid, smoke, or tear gas, but the result is the same: stun the target before you destroy it.

Windpipe

This has an obvious application. Control the air and you control the being. Hard strikes aren't needed here. One finger can do more damage than a fist on this target, because you will be hard-pressed to consistently fit a fist into every neck that threatens you. Striking the windpipe is often the best action in the first moment of combat. It makes a clear point and gives a slight opening. Keep on the neck if you can. No matter the size of the opponent, you can win with this target. A neck blow is a counter to every grab imaginable from the standing position. The neck is very open and very weak.

Carotid Artery

Striking the carotid artery can result in a knockout, because it delivers air to the brain. A great deal of power is needed to stun or damage an artery with blunt force, but it's more than conceivable and incredibly effective if you apply the butt end of a knife or your forearm. The arteries run down the neck from beneath the jawbone to the collarbone in a V shape. Your forearm should make contact just below where the jaw connects to the skull. The target should be immediately stunned and should pass out in the following second. Anchor the head if you aren't sure you can crank out enough power. Push the head to the side and slam the artery.

The method of countering this is taught in the basic boxing set; it is the forearm uppercut that connects to the chin. Be sure to advance during the technique so you can attain a ramming effect. What makes this effective is the fact that your hand covers the artery and other vitals in the area during the strike. Keep the hand flat and stretch it over every vital you can.

Top of the Spinal Column

This is the last inch of spine before it turns to skull. It's a very soft area and a high damage target. Striking here with solid technique shuts off the brain's connection to the body. The entire spinal column is a primary target. It immediately disables the fighter, if damaged.

Brachial Artery – Femoral Artery

I group these two together because the execution and effect are similar. Being struck in either target hard enough can result in a knock out. I've been struck in these targets before, and it's more than painful. It's like some horrible drug you wish you never took. The effect lasts between fifteen seconds to three minutes and does disable the fighter during that time.

There are two 'exposed' arteries in the arm: the brachial and lateral thoracic arteries. Striking in the center of the upper arm on either side will tag one of them. The brachial artery can also be struck from the bottom of the upper arm with a front kick or uppercut. No matter where you hit, the effect is similar so long as it's the center of the upper arm.

There are two points that the femoral artery can be tagged from. One point is just about an inch below the hip at the center of the front of the thigh. The other point is about two inches above the knee in the center of the front of the thigh.

Groin

A groin strike or kick doesn't disable a determined fighter. As the fighter becomes conditioned, the shock of impact disappears and eventually they will tell you they'd rather take a groin blow than a head shot. The groin is a lethal force strike, but you must leave that belief at the courthouse: In real life, there is no lethal force strike. People want to live and will do whatever it takes to maintain that status. They have weak points and by striking them you do wear the fighter down, but you won't put him down. That's where choking comes in.

When a kick or knee to the groin lands correctly, the attacker bends over. If your head is right in front of theirs, you will be in more pain than they were. Head bashes will knock out an average-sized man. Remember to move your head to the side when you strike the groin with your knee. If your nose gets broken, it's unlikely that it will heal properly: you might just be a freak for life. As your knee makes contact, align your head with his shoulder so that when his head flies forward, it doesn't fly into yours.

Knee

There's really only one way to break the knee in combat. Anchor their foot with yours and lean your knee into theirs. It works better than a kick and won't get you knocked down, either. This is a realistic technique and I hope you always think of it as primary. It implies a stalemate is going on, though, that both fighters are pushing against each other like Sumo wrestlers or that the opponent lacks a better reaction than just standing there long enough to get his knee broken. You won't often have time for this, but when you do, use it because it is devastating. An attacker will be debilitated. Kicks are functional but a bent knee cannot be severely damaged with a kick. The above technique forces the knee to straighten, allowing for a break.

Floating Ribs

The floating ribs are a source of many urban myths, one being that they aren't really attached and the others being too long to be worth mentioning. They are quite attached, but like the cork on a wine bottle, they're the weakest point. This is really the only torso target worth hitting. A freight train elbow will utterly destroy this target and likely land your opponent in critical condition. Dropping knees are also a great way to wreck this target; the rib will split off and dig into the vitals of your attacker.

Finding the Opportunity

It's not enough to train counters for each specific attack. This teaches you to counter impossible situations (which remain impossible with such a heavy approach) but not openings. An opening is much like an exit in a building; it's obvious and should you decide to decline it, you are less likely to get out of it. You don't want to be hung up on what the attack is or the general speed of the weapon. See the opening and react to it.

There is no set way to react to an opening. Therefore, this technique is built around action as opposed to response. A fighter sees the opening like a runner sees the finish line. It's part of the game and must be perceived in order to make a strong play. The second the opponent steps too far, you should have already acted on it and the fight should be over by the time the sentence ends. When you see the exit, don't hesitate.

Where the opportunity sleeps depends on the fighters involved, weapons involved, and special knowledge that includes environmental manipulation. Every situation is new and familiar at the same time. A certain degree of background knowledge must be carefully applied to a flowing nature in order to accurately perceive the situation. The true mystery is *how much* of *what* do you apply to *where*.

Have faith in your methods and don't get caught up with those questions. You already know how to act. This is the ultimate expression of multi-tasking, but in order to properly complete every task, you must not overthink any of them. Things come at you and you either have to deal with it as it comes, or destroy the source. Whatever you do, don't get caught up with one attack because another will follow. Keep it simple.

Chapter 8: Sparring Methods

Sparring is a serious part of training, but often schools get tunnel vision on one type and create a specialized fighter who cannot stand up to the varying pressures of real combat. To avoid this, and to make this book a little more effective, I have compiled the different kinds of sparring, and listed them by how much contact is involved.

A real fight is all the methods combined, but I want you to be able to understand how each general style warps the rules of engagement. These methods can be used with or without weapons and the numbers that can be involved are infinite.

Flow Sparring

This is the most basic sparring and is used to develop key combat reactions: advancing, retreating, evasion, and striking.

The nature of the method is not to hurt your opponent. There is no contact but there are clear hits. It teaches how to advance on openings without having to get hit and also builds a certain degree of trust between the sparring partners. Both must read the movement of the opponent and predict their actions. They must learn how to predict what the opponent expects, in order to effectively confuse and throw off the opponent.

This method is designed to give just enough ability and insight to move on to hard sparring, but without conditioning, it is of little use. You have to be able to give a decent punch (and take a decent punch) before even considering a friendly but painful match.

Hard Sparring

This can be done with or without protective gear and follows the same objective as flow sparring, except you'll actually get hit. There is no grabbing because it is based upon speed. If grappling were included, there would be less of an opportunity to practice footwork, and the fight would change direction. Keeping pace and wisely spending energy is the main issue when you get hit.

Grapple Sparring

There is no hitting in this method. Retreat is not a possibility, either. You and your opponent must get in full contact and use the weight and direction of the other to put him down.

From there, it's a way to practice submissions, chokes, and body manipulation. The method of winning here is to force the opponent to tap out.

Man Hunt Method

This is a way of practicing stealth technique in a realistic mode. Terrain can't be predicted and you have to learn to adjust to your environment quickly. The arena is as large or small as you want it to be. A house or the woods fits the general idea.

Countering your opponent can be seen as laying down loose stone, for example, around your area to undo his attempts to tread softly. The intent is to stalk and bring down the target without him becoming aware of your position.

Zombie Method

The zombie method requires a feeder and a receiver—an attacker and a defender. This method focuses on defense, and the intention is not to harm the attacker. A good way to envision this is to think of a drunken friend who's looking for a fight. The receiver can't attack and instead counters and defends against the zombie. When the zombie is "killed," it comes back to life, making this an endurance race, which the receiver is almost sure to lose. This method comes from the

Viking war systems and definitely improves your odds against one opponent. The only way to stop the zombie is by submission.

Pack Method

The pack method is just like an open battle charge. An even number of fighters are on each team, and they are each armed differently. There should be no limitation on the types of weapons to create varying challenges. This method teaches teamwork against a group, which can make all the difference in a fight.

If the other group is scattered, and can't work together, they have no chance. You must train with this method if you want to succeed in worst case scenarios.

Cornering Method

This has two intents: to make a single fighter more capable against multiple opponents, and, to make multiple opponents better at cornering a single person. Learning to work as a cohesive unit is key to defeating a single opponent. If the team can't work together, it's impossible for the single fighter to prevail.

Likewise, if a single person can throw the others into confusion by using their teammates as shields and keeping them from executing a solid plan, there is no way for the multiple opponents to succeed.

Chapter 9: On Facing Your Opponent

Neighborhood Rules

Indulgence is the worst plague to strike the human race. Its path can't be mapped, yet when we see it, indulgence is undeniably there. It doesn't hide, yet is careful not to charge. Our typical reaction to instinctive indulgence creates indecision, failure, and death; hence, bad reaction is our enemy and must be slaughtered. After that, there is no enemy. Hate is indulgence, and lack of clarity is lethal. We must preserve the solidity we create in peace so that it may be applied in war. This clarity and power can keep anything from doing you harm, and keeps you flexible enough that you know when to march and when to hold camp.

The idea is that we bring things to combat—which in this case is a situation in which an attacker compels you to protect yourself—yet take nothing from it. The first thing an average person takes from combat is fear, then anger, purpose, and finally the motivation to survive. The stages are all similar and can be seen as one.

The decisions made by a warrior should be made outside of war. If someone attacks you, perhaps attempts to mug you, there is no thinking, only doing. We must not make fixed decisions in a place so "un-fixed" that it seems limited; we must flow through hazard as it comes for us. There are thousands of conclusions to stop at, so why stop at death? If there are so many to choose from and so many chances to be wrong, why choose anything at all?

If you spend too much time on the question, you won't be able to give a conclusive, effective answer, and despite the effort you'll find yourself more confused. In life, this leads to answers. In combat, this leads to failure. We must not be caught up in the combat. We must become the combat and hence feel the answer. When you do this, the word *fight* disappears. Loss does not exist. We see action and react purely, without fear or anger, without indecision or honor.

The chemical change in the body is immense and when you face it for the first time, you'll say that it cannot be overridden and that it fully controls the fighter. It is true that there's no escaping what our system does to survive, but what we do to the system while surviving is different. The body knows the fight. The moment it begins, our eyes dilate and muscle convulsions in the form of twitching and a seemingly endless readiness for action takes over.

Fine motor skills vanish as adrenaline and animal instinct overpower the human factor. This, however, is where the uncontrollable stops. Emotion is the only controllable factor in this mess. But what one *can* control, another may be controlled *by*. Don't waste emotional energy on the target; they aren't human until after the fight.

I can only tell you the house is burning. It's up to you to leave.

The burning house is emotion. Should you allow it to scar your skin, you will live until you no longer believe in being burned or until there is no body left to torch. Until then, you should consider your position. You are alive until you are dead, and the moment you allow something to exist that doesn't perfectly reflect your situation, you muddle your existence. A muddled existence is one waiting to die.

The mind is a mirror; clean it every day. Clarity is what is set before you. Why it's set there is no more an issue than who put it there. The situation must be dealt with as it is, not as you wish it to be. Your opponent is a great enemy of no man; few hate him when the question is considered by him, hated by many when considered by you. Don't make a man of him.

Wreck the target and make it nothing more than that.

Chapter 10: A Final Lesson on Your Surroundings

Up to this point, the surroundings involved during a fight has not been a significant issue. Until now, the greatest related concern was whether or not you were standing or grounded. While this is the most important basic issue, it's only the tip of the iceberg. Superior force can be undone by a simple rise or fall in ground. Serious changes can cause concussion or death. Mastery of your surroundings is the final step to effective survival.

Types of Surroundings

Depending on how you position yourself in combat, you change your enemy's position. These things should not be randomly chosen. They should directly reflect the advantages and disadvantages of the ground under your feet.

There are two general rules that you must understand before entering combat. First, the ground is a neutral force.

Second, when the enemy understands it better than you do, it becomes an enemy force. These rules have two corollaries: you must know your ground if you are to fight on it, and you must attack it with the same vigor you do your target.

Stomp the ground like you mean to kill it. If you are marching on a steady incline or decline, walking through marsh, ice, snow or water, you don't walk like you're in an elementary school hallway. You plant your weight with intent to remain in position. If glass were under you, it would break. If ice were under you, you would not slide. If the ground rapidly went downward, you would hold traction because of the force you used to stay put.

Not only does stomping have this obvious practical application, it has a secondary psychological application. Any loud noises used against a shocked or fearful target hampers his ability to respond or act against an incoming attack.

All ***bumpy terrains*** fall into two categories: descending and ascending. They have the same effect but can lead to very different tactical responses. If your target hits a bump (ascending) and falls, he is going to land with his head higher than his feet in all likelihood. Despite this serious disadvantage, it is not nearly as bad as landing in a dip.

Should the opponent hit a dip (descending) he will land with his feet higher than his head. If injured or intoxicated, gravity will make getting back up significantly harder. Throughout this section, remember that the way to assault a fallen target is the same as standing—circle toward the back and hammer. Any place not defended is suitable.

There are generally two types of surroundings when it comes to *enclosed areas*: sitting and hallways. You can't maneuver and in the case of a chair, your only way back could injure your spine. No matter what, your objective is to reestablish distance. You must give yourself prior warning so that he isn't on you immediately, get distance and go from the sphere of influence (SOI).

Defensive surroundings have two things going for them: exits and cover. Again, you must position yourself properly. The cover needs to be between you and him and the exits must not leave the field of effect of the cover. There is little point in having cover if all you can do is stay there; you need a place to move to if outgunned.

Aggressive surroundings or terrain only concerns dips and humps, like the first section. The difference is the size. When I say humps, I mean fire hydrant-sized objects—benches, fallen trees, sidewalks, and other large fallen debris. Again, you must position your opponent relative to these natural weapons. If he winds up behind you, he may just rhino charge you into one.

Deadly surroundings were covered in the previous section: anything that compromises your ability to move, assert your power, draw a weapon or escape cuts your survival rates down to nil. This is why you disrupt your opponent instead of concentrating on destroying him; this is far more efficient. Once down, there's almost nothing you can do.

* * *

Combat is without rules or referees. Self-defense and protecting oneself from an unexpected attack is not like sparring in a controlled setting. Defending oneself in an urban setting could end with you being physically harmed—or worse.

Think you can't punch someone in the groin? You have to destroy the entire target if you are defending yourself and feel you are in enough danger that you must. The only thing you need is a realistic view of the situation and everything else will fall into place naturally.

Don't worry about the courts; your life is on the line right now. There is nothing wrong with pulling a knife on an aggressor if your life is at risk. There's no lack of honor in it because honor has already left with the arrival of an attacker who is threatening your existence.

These are the ground rules of survival:

Retreat if you are able to, because contacting local

authorities for help is better than getting into a fight that you aren't guaranteed to win.

If you are unable to retreat, use counter offensive technique, and only react to an attack in a way that seriously injures the attacker. The word *retreat* is without pure definition, however; it all depends on the situation. Think hard, clear, and fast.

The second rule is preparation. Train every day as though you were walking to your doom. When you leave the house, make sure you aren't missing a single piece of your toolbox. Knife, gun, keys, wallet, and everything you need to successfully survive in your environment. Watch the world closely and prepare accordingly. The only thing that can be seen as just as bad as being underprepared is being overprepared. Don't drown under your own weight.

Be alert, be awake. Let no one see your action unless they are taking part in it. When you walk into a room, see your enemy in the first five seconds and see every path to and from them. Exits, entrances, paths of attack and possible retreat (again, it depends on the situation). See absolutely everything.

The last ground rule is an ideal, but if you keep your head above water, it is much easier to attain than you might believe. Never fuck up—ever, ever, ever.

Do everything with clarity and conviction and never catch

yourself stuck in indecision or disbelief. Believe what you see and search out everything you don't.

The simplest part of combat is the bottom line: People don't attack bigger or stronger people than they are. Don't expect to be able to contain some random attacker you know nothing about. You never saw them before, and only have a second to see their targets. When that happens, your best bet is to get the hell out of the way and draw a weapon. You need aid and without it, you will be thrown into the unfathomable and the concrete.

Never take a risk or death will be right in front of you.

Part 2: Knives and the Sphere of Influence

When balancing your scales, seek wiser company than yourself.

— M. D. Holden

Chapter 11: The Modern Knife

This chapter is from an article written by the author, 08/22/2014.

It can kill what we eat, it can clean what we kill, it can prep what we cook and we can even eat with it. It can defend our lives, it can open our canned goods, it can cut stuck seat belts, and it can even whittle. There are no other tools that can say that. The knife is truly man's best friend.

This article will teach common sense—something sorely lacking where fighting knives are concerned. The weapon has been marginalized in favor of the gun and with it, the system for safely carrying, deploying, and applying the weapon.

I'd like readers to see how closely related the knife is to the gun. I would like them to stand in shock at how forgotten these ideas have become, as though the knife were never dangerous at all. My work has always concerned a knife and I have noticed numerous avoidable hazards born from ignorance.

A weapon is only a weapon if you can safely manage it. Otherwise, it's just a trap; a bomb with a hair trigger, just waiting for your stupidity to set it off. We all have stupid moments, but they need not get bigger or more numerous.

Etiquette

If you ever wonder how you should behave with a knife, just treat it as a gun. People don't like it when you brandish a gun casually or point it at them. The feeling is the same with a knife. If you work with one, don't leave it laying around open, or laying around at all.

It is my opinion that a person should never open carry. The element of surprise is one of the most important in application. Your opponent wants information about your weapons; they will naturally and inevitably seek it out. Even the untrained want to know. Never forget that inexperience doesn't mean a lack of instinct. Open carry makes it easier for your attacker to assess your abilities.

Never place something between the target and your weapon, like your empty hand. It seems far-fetched to people who have never been subjected to high stress, but there actually is a chance—slim or great, depending on your teacher—of impaling your hand with the knife. Let them occupy different places: one hand high or low during the attack depending on the blade's position, or just keep the knife in the lead as much as possible.

No matter how much you train, your hands are better known by your body than your blade. Under stress, you may forget your training. A simple rule, like keeping the knife in front or on a different line than your empty hand, can be life saving. It's easier than trying to program complex drills and apply them to a threat.

In any tool, quality is most important. One thing a knife has in common with a gun or a car is that new doesn't mean good. Don't be obsessed with a factory edge. Be obsessed with learning to sharpen and maintain a knife. Steel quality is subjective. Analyze what you need the tool for, and make it meet combat requirements without losing too much of its daily ability.

I once saw a group of whitewater rafters choose chromium blades for their superior edge. The edge was so needed in that situation that its tendency to rust was ignored. They balanced the scales of logic and chromium won. When balancing your scales, seek wiser company than yourself.

It's nice to like your local law enforcement. It's impossible to do so if you're afraid of them. Having a legal knife may not always be convenient but it does make life easier. One way to make an oversized or tactical knife more acceptable is to use it. Worn, work knives do not raise the ire of the law. But worn does not mean battered. The image you should exude is one of skill and respect—for the weapon and for others.

Daily Carry

Daily carry is a serious choice. Over time, the physical and psychological ramifications of this comfort can actually bother you. But having picked your weapon, you probably already understand that it's an acceptable caveat when stacked against being dead or victimized until dead.

The safest place a weapon can be is on the person. Saying you carry daily should mean you carry on your person, in the car, in the house, in the bathroom, and in bed. If these carry positions have to change, you must train to accommodate that change. If your pants are across the room when you're in the shower, think: "Is the weapon closer to me or the door?" If the answer is the door, change it!

Over time, the prefix 'daily' becomes a little more apparent. When I was thirteen, I carried something slow and useful: a multi-tool. When I was fifteen, I carried something flashy: a balisong. By fifteen and a half, the world had broken my Bali and an altercation forced me to never carry one again. I then carried a fixed blade M-Tech.

Since then, little has changed. My current carry tool is sub-hilt, having learned knives can be pulled out by force during cutting. It has a bigger belly to accommodate my work and a not so acute tip to stand to the pressures of that work.

Daily will change you. Carry will change you. Both of these will change your knife and if everything goes in the right direction, you will have all your fingers, toes, and eyes and you won't be in jail. Take this seriously, and get others to take this seriously. The only difference between a knife and a gun is range.

Accessibility is a major concern. The best example is frontline soldiers—safeties off, rifles slung but ready. This is the pinnacle of accessibility, when the tool is already in your hand. This is a method seldom attained with a knife, though it is a must with mace or a flashlight.

It's impossible to make any weapon perfectly accessible when concealed rather than in hand. The trick is to never allow more than two steps to be in your process—like ankle carry. I clear the cover and draw just the same, but I have to drop first. It can be made simple. It can be made fast, but better on the belt line.

A weapon is not necessarily comfortable, but it's comforting. Before complaining about the wear on your jeans or the stickiness between your holster and hip, remember that perfect comfort is not the main goal, but it's a concern. There are two kinds of comfort. The weapon must be close to the body, retained in its holster hard enough that you can't shake it out and if it must be secured to your pants, so be it.

However, if it's so close to your body that your checkered grips are taking off skin, or your knife clip can't clear your pants without practically taking a piece with it, this is also wrong. You won't get an 'A' in both forms of comfort, so shoot for a solid 'B' in both fields. If anyone takes issue with such underachieving, remember that we are living by limited means in a limited universe. We make the best out of what we have.

The final subject to discuss is the law and how we permit it to affect our carry. We would all rather be judged by twelve than carried by six, but there's the ludicrous side of this, too. We can all hear the echoes of that sentence spilling from the mouths of the carriers of excessive force. They break the jaw of a loudmouth in a bus station—"Well, rather be judged by..." We get it. You're going to jail anyway, asshole.

When I carried tactical folders, I dressed for excess. Four inches was the minimum. Most of my conduct was acceptable, but when it wasn't, the hood of my car looked like a knife store. Never was one confiscated and all of them were technically illegal. In my opinion, several things were on my side.

1) I worked with my knives, and they all showed signs of wear and excellent maintenance.

2) I treated the officers as what they are—keepers of the system that protects us from predators.

3) I'm not a violent criminal, which always helps.

So, in my private life, the knife itself hasn't been important in how the law judged me.

My conduct determined how I was treated. A combat situation isn't like this, however. When you make bodies, there will be cameras, there will be juries, and there will be consequences. Even the style of knife you carry will be used to judge you.

Taking all of this into account, let's say my knives weren't on the door, in the glove box, middle console, and on my hip. Let's say one was stuck to the visor, one jutting out from the middle of the console and the seat, and one strapped to my ankle. I'd look like a mall ninja, an idiot and an eventual criminal. No matter how nicely I treat them, I'm getting the worst they have to offer.

Concealment

Concealment is an art. Specifically, the art of controlled disadvantage: you are installing one advantage (surprise) at the expense of another (accessibility). When this goes wrong, you typically hear something like, "I sure was surprised when I couldn't access my weapon in time. How long will these stitches take?"

Surprise and accessibility worked for your opponent that time. With a little thought and trouble, it doesn't have to be that way.

Concealment deals with so many variables that I consider it an advanced skill. Rather, I think of it as an advanced application of common sense. Veteran police officers still find ways to make producing their weapon more efficient without reducing accessibility or surprise. These are people whose jobs depend on their side-arms. We can learn from them.

Concealment in terms of weapons basically means having a cover garment. This adds a second step in the already daunting task of presenting your weapon. First, your hand goes there, then it clears the cover garment, then the weapon hand draws. This is hard and it takes time. We aren't even dealing with lowering the center of gravity, the *En Garde*, or what to do with your empty hand.

Train logically. Take for instance veteran police experience: they used to teach point shooting starting hands at the sides, and now some of the trainers know better. As it happens, when an officer is assaulted, he brings up his guard instinctively. Even if you're being shot at and on the run, odds are you're covering your head while you do that instinctively.

Bearing these particulars, one should practice their draw from a covered position as well as from a natural position. More so, the weapon needs to be kept in a reasonable location. Ankle carry goes out immediately—bad enough being forced to clear a pant leg, now you have to stop running and crouch. For a tertiary it isn't so bad, but if you need it now, keep it on the belt line.

The Guard

I'm sure everyone above five has a good idea of what a classic *En Garde* stance is. Maybe you grew up with Tyson on TV or Chuck Norris. Any photo I put up would do exactly as much justice as that hazy memory, however. The guard is learned, not imitated. Conceptually, it ideally covers the face and throat, with an ability to roam down to the sternum. Practically, the best way to do this is to punch your opponent in the face, though you may be hard pressed to call that a guard.

Self-protection should be dynamic and counter offensive—not simply with your hands up, but covering and dominating the line of attack (the shortest distance between you and your opponent). Acting first is the best guard (circling to the outside). When that fails, keep your hands above his. This gives you a better shot at getting to his face first, in the event of attack.

The knees should be bent and the center of gravity should be as low as possible without restricting the ability to move in any direction and with little to no telegraphing. The jaw should be turned downward to protect the throat. Nothing else requires alteration if you act first.

Basic Capabilities

Initially, this was to be called *Basic Skills*, but this isn't basic. Putting steel on target requires timing, sensitivity, will to act, and serious training. The only way I could keep the word in the title is to speak of the weapon's *basic capability* and not the *combatant's*. We already talked about what is efficient. Now we get into the contextual parts.

Each tool has its strong and weak sides. A forward thrust is almost always the answer, but not if you have a clinch pick or another exclusively icepick-grip weapon. The more obtuse the weapon, the harder it becomes to attack at a straight, true angle. Sometimes the solution becomes aiming slightly to the side of the target in order to achieve deep, fight-ending wounds.

Thrusting: Like anything else in combat, you have to mind your guard—especially your legs. Body weight powers this but it should be in sync with your arm. When one piece falls behind the other we get inefficient and cumbersome.

Planting the weight in the rear leg, push forward and thrust to the full extension of the arm. This should be followed up by rapid stabs to vital areas while grounding your opponent.

Pecking: A thrust with no body weight behind it. The peck is a flail, a jab but with the point end narrower than your fist. It keeps the enemy away. Very little use in life or death struggles, but needed in dueling and sparring.

Slashing: A long-range technique, since it requires timing and the weapon is not already lined up with the opponent. It rakes in nature, with the front of the blade leading. It cuts clean and deep, severing nerves. Blood loss will be the X factor as the pain isn't likely to be enough to stop them.

Consider the inefficiency of the slash. It has practical limitations. I travel to point B in order to hit the opponent. There is no way to slash from point A. If he does not do what you expect, this could be the last thing you do on this earth. As a part of a retreating measure—in theory—it can neutralize the hand, but missing the target makes you dead and not cutting deeply enough makes you dead.

Sawing: An anti-choke or grapple measure. Rapidly sawing arms will free you up even when pitted against a leather clad opponent. Serrations—good ones—are required material.

Tearing: A mixture of thrusting and cutting. When the blade is inserted into the target, it is followed up by tearing it out instead of pulling. The blade can be turned to maximize damage; such a turn makes the wound difficult if not impossible to close. When you tear, you are not only pulling it out, but pulling it or pushing it to the side to create a deep, wide open channel that may kill. An unintended consequence is that his body will go whichever way you push while that knife is in him; this is the ultimate in pain compliance.

Ripping: A method common to improvised and primitive weapons. The intent is to create a shallow wound, setting off but not severing as many nerves as one could with sharpened steel. Cumulative damage is not something you walk out the door with but something you are forced to rely on should equipment fail.

Hammering: This consists of beating someone with a blunt portion of the knife, such as the handle or flat side of the blade. This application comes out more commonly with flashlights as it's technically a step back on the force continuum where knives are concerned.

Hacking: A fine motor skill technique that becomes easier the heavier the tip of your blade is. The blade is sent down and whipped back up. It is very effective against enemy fingers that come in range of your blade.

Basic Theory

I've had three distinct martial flavors in my life. The taste was in how they taught students to stand and move. The first was a sword based martial art with an empty hand practice. Since the sword is at the front of the practice, the footwork and stance reflects that. On the clock, their lead foot would be at twelve and the rear at six. This creates a thin profile which leaves less to hit, but makes the balance weak from any other position aside from twelve and six.

My next taste was American Karate with teachers that match your stereotypical law enforcement and self-defense profile. Their interpretation was good, but fell short in the end. Because they favored unarmed combat, they require a stronger stance that can handle more dynamic pressure. They stood with the lead foot between eleven and twelve, the rear at five with the enemy positioned at twelve.

Then along came Wing Chun, which is the operating method behind this project. Though we often use a stance like the Karate schools, we face, with both shoulders at equal distance from the target. This concept of equal distance allows for more rapid attacks across greater target areas in less time without violating a person's natural tendency to face a threat.

Classical Korean and Japanese martial artists stand bladed to create a smaller target area. While making one safer from the initial blow, it lacks follow-up ability and offensive techniques. While I do prefer to stand medial as opposed to lateral, all methods potentially add worlds of insight to your training.

In the event of ambush, there isn't any time to do anything except drop your center of gravity and act—no lead and rear foot. If you do have time, don't waste it getting into your favorite stance: use the space to move and escape if possible. If not, use the time to move into a better position to attack or counter his attack.

Training Methods

A *waster* is the term for a wooden training sword. You can use either a wooden sword or wooden knife for training and sparring. There is nothing you need to do more to prepare yourself than to hit something exceptionally hard. Since you won't be using your empty hand, you can use a tree if needed. This is a helpful tool in bringing you to understand that you need to grip the knife tightly; you will slip and you must learn to minimize that.

Train with both hands, use rounds and experiment vigorously. Use motor oil when you become more familiar.

It's as slippery as sweat or blood, and cheaper. The trick of learning to grip something tightly and still maintain reasonably relaxed reflexes comes with time and effort. Don't be frustrated when you hit a wall; they never stop, so get used to it.

Optional Tools

A similarity in all the subjects below is the eyes. Eye protection for yourself—and a means of destroying, limiting or distracting your opponent's eyes—helps an altercation from turning into a knife fight or simply being butchered. Cut-resistant clothing is handy but relative to your climate. This project doesn't deal with the relative—only the basic, only the true.

Relative things include improvised defense and job related required adjustments. I say improvised because bucklers and armor are obsolete. The closest you can get in a pinch is a towel wrapped around your forearm or *TIME* magazine taped in your sleeve. Because it all comes together so quickly, you can't protect both arms.

Consider this: Blood is slippery. If your off-hand gets wet due to injury, it won't be able to reliably keep enemy hands still. Even a watch can help to hold an arm still under slippery conditions, though it does take training. The increase in traction can be life-saving and any coverage on the artery is a good thing.

Job specific issues can range from a ban on some weapon use, to a mandate that only one weapon type be used, or none at all. This should widen your gaze in the martial arts if nothing else. Many tools are available everywhere, but you must be able to see them and then you must be able to use them.

Protecting your eyes from blood, concrete chunks, or any other detritus is common sense. Have military or at least sport grade glasses if you think any of this is worth investing a penny in. It isn't enough to count on your natural instinct when problems fly at over six hundred feet per second.

When you can't see, you need illumination. When you don't want them to see, you need illumination. Flashlights are required material on a planet with a setting sun: maintain one until this is no longer true. But remember that in the dark, it isn't brightness that matters—just having it. In the lowest low light conditions, a candle is bright. You don't need a flood light, just something light enough to carry every day that won't become a nuisance.

In the day, mace can be handy, but wind is its worst enemy and it can pollute whole buildings should you fire it inside. It also doesn't deliver consistency, which is the one thing we want in our carry tools.

In my old age, I may carry mace instead of a knife; I may not wish to lean on my physical ability so much, but for now I do, and mace isn't as dependable as my hands and not even close to my steel.

Getting back to judgment. It's all person to person. Some people like .380, some 9 millimeter and some .45. None of them are wrong. How much recoil do you want? How many bullets do you need?

These questions are subjective, intensely personal choices that we bet it all on, every day. Make your choices carefully and always, *always* seek a second opinion.

Chapter 12: Basic Targeting System, Edged Stage

Neighborhood Rules

For a while, I used several blade styles to express edged combat, but for the purpose of realism I settled on the ***C.C.B. (Common Carry Blade)*** which is at the core of this writing. Common carry blades are those without hand guards, with a blade under four inches. They are easy to conceal, and they shouldn't be used in standard grip. At first, it gives you the impression of just being a knife with virtually no other purpose, but after a while, all that changes. In truth, it's a hand enhancer and its prowess in close quarter combat takes most of the pure edged technique and changes it into boxing technique with a brutal bonus.

Any weapon must begin with the basic angles of attack. This weapon is more focused on its application, however.

There are eight angles: the two vertical angles, the two diagonal, the two opposing those, and the horizontal angles with that. Unfortunately, only six of those angles are truly useful; the vertical angles are incredibly limited but you'll know when they apply. The true concern is how you apply that to the muscle, tendon, and skin targets. This is expressed through counter offensive technique which revisits evasive footwork and for a short while teaches pure retreating technique through it is against the general strategy. The point of this is to teach rhythm with a blade. With more length, this is simple but once the weapon becomes a true extension of the hand, it becomes more complex due to the realization that you are three inches away from losing your thumb. The best way to get past this is to close range and do it quickly and decisively.

The next stage is ***C.Q.T.*** or ***Close Quarter Termination***. It is the combinations and footwork version of the boxing section. Primarily, it's thought-based instead of based in repetitive training. Technique is expanded only when the student has readied themselves in the previous technique. That means they must be able to see all their open targets. After that, they can forget it like yesterday's news. Control of the weapon hand is secondary to destruction of both hands. Though, eventually, it does deal with control as a general issue.

Your main objective is wrecking everything the target shoots at you. You only deal with core targets once every extremity has been dealt with.

Overview of Blade Technique

1. Counter Offensive
    - a.) Basic angles of attack
    - b.) Reintroduction to footwork
    - c.) Where to tag and why
    - d.) Unarmored points of attack
2. Close Quarter Termination
    - a.) Disabling the extensions of the body
    - b.) Destroying the body at the weakest points
    - c.) Shutting down the body in general (core targets)

Chapter 13: Short Range Knives and Puppet Theory

Neighborhood Rules

The ***sphere of influence*** is the exact range you can control without moving. For an unarmed combatant: it is the length of your arm. In terms of the armed combatant: it is the length of your weapon. With a baton, mace, knife or hand enhancer, this is fairly straightforward. With a pistol or rifle, it's something gained with experience. The effective range of your weapon depends upon skill: how fast you can move, how well you can predict the wind, and how well you can predict your opponent. Its true application is not an expression of facts, but of skill.

Moving Into Attack Range

Knowing when to move in self-defense is a lot like playing an instrument with new musicians: you have to play the right notes at the right time. Not doing so can result in disharmony. You will make mistakes; it's a matter of making sure they aren't detectable or fatal. Watch his weapon. If it moves low, attack high. If it moves high, attack low. Some may be concerned about baiting or faking a blow. Remember that he's not looking for points; he is trying to kill you.

Your body must follow your weapon. If your weapon goes low, your torso and head follows. If your weapon goes high, you jump and follow the weapon down. Always follow your plan.

Even if he does fake a blow, by the time he fully extends, you have already struck your target. Afterward, he no longer has the will to strike you. He only has the power to react to pain. He can flail and cut your skin or thrust into you. The thrust will drag out before it penetrates vitals, and the cut will, too. It may be long, but it will be shallow. He is moving back: not downward, upward, or forward. The energy to attack is lost in the primitive desire to escape the pain which you've caused.

The idea is that he may panic at your moment of contact and miss entirely. More often than not, his response will be closer to panic and retreat rather than retreat and a counter cut. The instinct to protect one's life is not learned. It's instinct. Even the most honored soldier will care more about the knife against his balls than the mission in the moment: before the shock leaves him, assault.

When to Defend

The middle is the one area where a counter-attack becomes a counter: you can't outmaneuver a weapon in that battleground without making contact and redirecting the enemy weapon. This is the area which requires the most skill because there is no good place to evade to: the enemy weapon must be dealt with before all else.

In order to do this, you must control the distance. The effective range of his weapon becomes extremely important: you must be just outside of his range *plus* **a step** in order to effectively predict where the weapon will be when he hits your sphere of influence (SOI).

He steps to attack, and you see which foot is in the lead. You see which side the weapon hand is coming from, and you act accordingly. In order to defend, you need this space to remove accidents from the game plan. If you don't have it, your only option is to vigorously and violently assault the opponent until he gives you that space, or to retreat.

Remember that if you go too far back, you invite your opponent to go into combinations. Once the weapon starts moving, and changing locations, you may not be able to predict where and when it will strike. At one step away, I know where that weapon will hit if he's trying to kill me. Farther away, he will gain mental control over his emotions and begin to strategize. When this occurs, it's wise to do one of two things: Run like hell, or throw your weapon at him and run like hell.

Recapitulation

Attacking

1. See what the weapon is

2. High or low?

3. Attack the moment you feel his weapon moving

4. Attack at the position which is not defended: high, low. Low, high.

Defending

1. Be at the exact limits of the weapon, plus one step back.

2. Concentrate on handling the weapon as well as outmaneuvering.

3. If you can't maintain the distance, attack.

4. If you can't control the distance; throw it and run. (Be good at throwing and better at running.)

When *closer* to the target, you must further understand the tools you're dealing with. Either you have a badly made knife, or you have a weapon capable of shearing through clothing, then skin, then meat. If you have the first, then you have one target: open skin. A man in shorts gets it in the muscles near the shin or the tendon on the side of the knee. Attacking the groin isn't functional because of the penetration required to do damage. Should you attack this target or one like it, his weapon will be four inches into your lung before he feels the prick on his prick.

On the upper body, you hit the inside of his arms or his neck and face. Strike something he feels immediately, always open skin.

Should an amateur find themselves in the company of a fine blade, they should attack open skin as well. Even though they are holding good, sharpened steel, they still lack the presence of mind, accuracy and power to hit more difficult targets.

In an expert's hands, a hard reverse slash to the groin shreds everything in its path. He will jump back so fast and hard that no counter is possible. From the top, if you thrust into his collar bone on the side he carries his weapon, he will have no capability to attack. Both are fight-enders and both are almost non-lethal—if he makes it to a hospital in time.

Targeting and Puppet Theory

In a fight, it's important that you move fast. The moment things change, you have to react within the same breath. There can be no hesitation or ignorance, because both are lethal. When you see one of these basic targets opening, your intent should be to irradiate it.

My approach is something I call ***Puppet Theory.*** I call it a theory because a man can be right only until he is proven wrong. There will be unfathomable changes in each opponent and one never knows just how different they will be. To help reduce this possibility, I have developed this approach from objective fact and targets, while applying a common carry blade, which is most applicable to slashing. Therefore, when under attack, tendons and arteries are the main targets.

Tendons run through the neck and every limb. Cutting a tendon severs whatever is on the other end of it. This is why I call it Puppet Theory. Cut the tendons on the inner elbow and the wrists, and the ability is cut down. Cut the tendons on the wrist and the fingers are shut off.

I like this approach because it ends the attack but isn't likely to cause death. It also takes far too much time to kill. You may not be sure if you tagged the organ, and the gap of time that creates is an opening for another opponent. Cutting through a target takes a fraction of that time. Because it doesn't dig in like a thrust, it doesn't have to be pulled back from that direction, leaving room for technique that flows into technique, instead of linear movement better served against a single opponent.

Every limb has tendons. Striking a tendon is like severing the mind's control of the body without getting anywhere near the mind. It is a surgical strike that shuts down the targeted body part without killing, effectively ending the battle.

* * *

Most people have little experience with short-range weapons. They try to apply techniques that cannot and will not work, but it's so wired into their approach that they can't help themselves. Please use your head. Look at each weapon when you pick it up, feel the weight, and learn the grip. Look at the design and know your world. Do not insist that ignorance is really truth. You'd be better off convinced that the truth is constantly a lie.

A technique that requires the weight of the knife to cut or a loose grip has nothing to do with knives, yet I know several people who have that wiring. I can only hope the best for them, as no knife would guarantee that in their hands. There's also the reaction to use it as a blocking body in some, but when the blade stops in range of the opponent's weapon, the hand behind it will be cut. A short range weapon cannot block. This is a highly physical weapon, just as ugly and confusing as an unarmed fight. You slash hard and thrust *through* when you really want to get it done. There is nothing soft or safe about knives, and no matter what weapon you have, the combat ends the same.

The application is simple. When your blade meets the target, you should be intending to cut through the target. When you find an opening, thrust hard. This also applies to secondary striking, either with the hands or with the blunt parts of the knife; when you hit, you must hit as hard as possible.

This isn't a shitty fifties switchblade movie, or what one might think of as an honorable duel. Combat is sloppy, disgusting, and nobody looks good afterward. When you use a short-range weapon, everything becomes personal, but is much messier than an unarmed fight. A knife takes a great amount of mental and physical preparation to apply in combat.

* * *

The most important detail in any **_grip_** is that you don't loosen it for any reason. Fights don't end until everyone stops twitching, so there's never any reason to relax. If someone else gets their hands on that knife, you're in trouble. If you just drop the knife, you're still in trouble. You tried to attack someone, and now you're on even ground with them. It is a terrible situation. Hang on to that blade like it's the only thing keeping you alive, because that is likely to be true. Do not lose your blade.

Base is how attached you are to the ground, in a nutshell. The more of you is on the ground, the harder you'll be to manipulate. If one foot is off the ground, you can be pushed over, if both feet are off the ground you can be caught and thrown. In a street fight, one of the first things that happens aside from a haymaker (most common strike thrown by unschooled fighters) is closing range and getting incredibly physical. You want as much base as you can muster or you're living in a body bag.

Preserving base is your general objective in a fight. If not, you will be knocked to the ground and stomped into critical condition. At short range, it is absolutely imperative that you keep both feet on the ground. What that means during an attack is that you must make sure that your back foot stays planted when you lean into a strike. What that means on the retreat is that you have to match speed with the opponent so that you don't fall behind and stumble before getting into the target.

Treat combat technique like lightning; energy flows

through the point of least resistance, so your punches will be more powerful if the technique is grounded (or if the circuit is connected) by both your feet. The moment you take your foot off the ground, half of your power is sapped. You can be pulled, pushed, or killed while minor resistance remains your only friend. Only move when the moment says go, only attack when the opening presents itself, and only block when the strike is in range.

When I speak of base, it's important that I clarify how primary it is in survival. There's no time to retreat in most fights. It happens and you'd better be ready to roll. You are fighting mass with mass; you have to be connected to the ground as much as possible. Of course, there's never only one way to get 'er done. In this case the only thing you have to avoid is being in the middle. Make things difficult for the enemy.

Snapping Technique

In *snapping technique*, the idea is that your strike cannot be manipulated because the moment it makes contact is the moment it pulls back. If you don't meet a few general guidelines, it won't be powerful, however. First the strike must maintain contact with the target for about a half a second to fully transmit the force and as an easy way to assure this, you must aim beyond the target and pull back at that point, which is about four inches behind the target area. The theory behind snapping technique is that it gives the opponent little opportunity to retreat. With a typical punch, the target will be pushed back on contact. Because the target moves with the force, the strike only damages the exterior. Because a snapping strike doesn't follow through, the target won't move as much, and it creates more internal damage than external.

The application of snapping technique, when applied to a handheld weapon, is used to take away the likelihood that the opponent would get his hands on your knife hand. When applying snapping technique with an edged weapon, there is less need to hold to the target for that half a second. Because you are pulling back, it won't do lethal damage anyway and because there's no blunt force to transmit, you can't do more damage unless you use a follow-up strike. Faking thrusts is a good way to force the enemy to advance. Snapping technique is key here if you want to prod the target's mind.

Application Against Multiple Opponents

A technique designed to work against one opponent will utterly fail against two; your intent must go from killing to disabling in order to stay alive. The point of the form used in this method is to improve cutting technique and to teach targets. You should go after the targets available with the strikes available.

When fighting two opponents, you must divide your attention between them. Get tunnel vision on one, and you can expect a knife from the other. Cut one, then cut the other; keep doing it until neither of them are fit to fight. Never try to kill a man in battle. Only try to take away his ability to fight. When the fog has cleared, you can then decide what you will do.

Obviously, killing someone after the battle is pointless, unless a war surrounds it. Always consider the ripple effect, but most importantly, always know that protecting your life implies putting it even before killing the enemy. Killing takes minutes, which the other fighters will use against you. You only want to do fast damage; just enough to give you time to get at the others. Soon they will be bleeding too hard to fight or escape. Then you will have won the battle.

The thing with multiple opponents is that their entire strategy relies on surrounding you. They know you can't take on the strength and power of multiple people, so you have to think efficiently. Charge one at a time; make him retreat and punch a hole in their circle. Try to avoid fighting two at a time. Take the weakest and then move up the chain. They want you to take them on from your sides, where your sight is weakest and perception holds more power than intuition or intelligence. Always take them on at your strongest point and make sure that your weakest point is always moving away from them.

Multiple Attackers

There are three concerns in this situation. Your people, their people, and the numbers of both parties. The tactics change depending on if you're alone or if the target is; confusion erupts if you can't keep a solid command over your units. Everyone has to understand tactics if they are to fight with you. If they don't understand, they'll get in the way, get you hurt, and get themselves hurt. Understanding the game also comes into play when you're cornered. You can wreck their organization and take down three of them at a time simply because you know how to put them in each other's way.

Taking down one at a time is not ideal when you're cornered because once you get involved with one, you will have another coming at you almost instantly. It becomes more about evasion than decimation but the end result is the same if it's successfully applied. In a way you are using their energy against them but the execution is more than that because you're dealing with multiple attackers. Evade the first only when you can send him into the second, and so on. If the others aren't attacking, then you do have an opportunity to do serious harm, but don't get too involved; don't try to finish the target, only wound him. Ensure that you do structural damage with a blunt weapon as they aren't good for much else. When the target returns, you need to be sure they won't be able to charge as solidly or strike as strongly.

A good example of a disorganized attack is if three units are charging you. Let's say the first is facing you and attempts a roundhouse swing to the temple with a bat, the second target is at your right shoulder and is just about to get their hands on you while the third is approaching from your back with a knife. As target one swings, you duck and he strikes target two. You come around behind target two before target three can get to you and lock around his neck using him as a human shield against target three. This is how quickly things can go wrong even if you have two people helping you. One slip, one trip, and all of you are dead.

The biggest problem in that scenario is that one and two were aiming for your head while three was aiming for your upper torso. They didn't think about what they were attempting to accomplish and it cost them their victory. One was correct in aiming for the head since he was the first to attempt contact. Two was stupid because the head was already a taken target. Due to his position and timing, he should have been attacking the knee. Three was correct to take the center of mass because he is the last to make contact, and so should take the strongest area. One idiot is all it takes. One blind stupid jackass can get three people killed in less than five seconds. When someone volunteers to fight with you but hasn't ever trained with you, just tell him to hang back or go home because he's useless to you.

From here, you can either have him entice the target to charge him by verbal encouragement, or just have him pull a knife so that the problem is distracted from the other two. The remaining two units flank the target while the third just tries to get the attention of the target. The only true method to attack in this case is to have one charge the knees while the other takes the head. The center of mass is too well-defended to be a target yet.

The next thing to deal with is being cornered by over four people which is a good situation for you and a terrible situation for them, believe it or not. There is no way to make all those people into a cohesive unit because there are more people than targets on your body now. Escalation is your best friend; if you have a gun or knife, then use it. Create as much battle shock as you can in the minds of your targets or attackers.

When over two attack at once, your only hope is their

timing. Use every gap to put one in the other's way. When the first target charges you, send him into the second. In order to defeat them, work with the gaps in the charges each target takes. You can't defeat them all by direct confrontation.

Knife Sparring and Knife Combat

It is important that you are as realistic as possible. Knife fighting is hell and no sugar coated training method will prepare you.

Every strike has to be hard and fast without compassion for the sparring partner. Try not to hurt each other, but don't look out for each other, either. It is still a slow second to the real thing, but this method increases endurance in every form of combat. It dulls the nerves a great deal and prepares the mind and body for full-force combat.

When someone says ***knife fighting***, their head is often drawn to scenes of movies, scenarios from the ego and illusion in general. In each of these delusions (in "normal" people) there is often the concept of defense, that they're using a knife to protect their own lives. But like a wrench protecting the interest of the bolt, a knife can only protect another material interest. And so, our primary response is to defend them when they are assaulted. When such a thing is threatened—such as in the case of an intruder entering a home—we spring into action and draw our weapons. We prepare ourselves to defend our external interests by attacking the attacker of our possessions.

When defending the self comes into question, the rules change in incredible ways. There is no way to see such a attack before it happens, so we must simply react. If we attempt to reach for help by drawing a weapon, we may be killed. We must not be distracted from the problem. We must move out of its way before we can draw.

Once you have drawn your weapon, you are the attacker. You are destroying the problem in the most efficient way possible. I see no problem with this, but it's important that a knife fighter understands where defense ends (after the first strike) and where the attack begins (the moment the blade is drawn).

When we discuss protecting ourselves against sudden and possibly lethal attacks, it's probably unlikely we'll have time to draw a knife, and even less likely that we can use that knife effectively when caught by surprise.

Chapter 14: The Pennsylvania Knife

This article was previously published September 26, 2014 on the Blade Ops blog.

In every facet of every society, the knife has been and continues to be an incredibly important part of every person's life. Like fire, you just can't live well without it. They are so prevalent they are mostly ignored, leaving an enormous knowledge gap that can only exist in a complacent society that thinks close combat is a thing of the past and that a knife's only job is cutting tomatoes.

Funny thing is people still find themselves whittling and cutting toward themselves or working in close quarters and cutting toward their body. The knife demands respect and the consequences of disrespect are maiming and death. It's still a seatbelt cutter, still a pry bar, and still your last best hope where a gun can't go.

There are many knives in my social circle. I'd describe my

area as a Kershaw or Kabar kind of place. These wouldn't be my first choice but they're stout enough blades for the work we do, and typically, your work is the key factor in your knife choices if any true labor is involved. Ninety percent of these knives are dull—with crusty, gritty innards and slippery handles—held lazily and used carelessly with few exceptions.

All tools, especially those you carry, should be maintained as well as your car or gun and should be used with just as much care. This treatise exists to help cure the blind spot in our culture. This is less about martial technique and more just a short work on what a long-term relationship with a good tool should look like.

If a Kali or Silat practitioner happens to stumble upon this, consider we don't have that here right now. We have a knife culture, but it's not an educated one and that needs to change. Many of these people don't leave themselves the time to commit to learning in person and this may well be the closest some get to understanding how to use a knife in the gravest extremes.

I have over ten years of uninterrupted martial training, first in a Korean strike based system, then in Wing Chun. Before WC, I ran the knife through the Korean system (Shim Gum Do) and now, I run it through the WC system. Even before I trained, I was trying to find these solutions and stumbled across a lot of knife fighting data from then to now. I always had a partner to work the concepts with and after ten plus years of banging my head against a wall, I feel like I know what I'm talking about to the extent of what I'm going to share.

I've called this project the *Pennsylvania Knife* because this is the result of growing up in Pa., having access to tons of knives, but zero knife fighting schools. This is no more than incredibly important bare bones information. If I had a school, I'd leave it up to my Sifu. If I could find a school, I'd just tell people to visit, but we just haven't got it yet. So, here we are.

Knife Maintenance

Very few knife smiths are left in the world. You are unlikely to send your knife away for a check-up; it's at once too important to send away and not important enough to spend a third of the cost to keep it in fighting shape. For dependable results, learn to do it yourself.

The first aspect is sharpening, something you can't just automatically do perfectly. Some commonly available kits look impressive and intuitive, and my friends have fine results with them without much practice. Myself, I only use an oil stone and fine grit sand paper.

Should you choose the more old-fashioned method and have no one to teach you, practice on something you don't like for a while. Remember that steel is not created equal: 440 tool steel and AUS8A won't sharpen the same way. Practice applying the knife to the stone smoothly and consistently, maintaining the same angle throughout.

The next aspect is breakdown. You should be able to convert your knife to a pile of screws and plates with little difficulty. In the long term, this means that screws will need to be replaced as they inevitably strip. The reason for this total breakdown is to oil and clean every little corner of the tool. This might seem silly, but corrosion is measured in months, not minutes, and beauty is maintained over time, not something that simply is.

Unless I have a lot of free time, I typically don't strip my knife until I hear a creak when I open it. This extends the life of your screws, and a little squeaking for a day won't break anything.

Some parts of your knife don't need to be oiled or cleaned. For these, the smartest solution is putting superglue on the threads of the screws to ensure that nothing loosens over time and then simply never touching them again.

Some damage can't be fixed by an oil stone. Nicks or broken tips need to be ground out with a file. This file needs to be maintained with a wire brush to clear the metal shavings. So far, my kit is stone, oil, special screw drivers, extra screws, superglue and now even the wire brush. If I hadn't inherited this stuff—minus the glue, screws and oil—I'd have already spent as much on the kit as the blade.

There is nothing casual about this. I didn't choose it casually, don't carry it casually, and I don't maintain it casually. Each tool has its own needs which you will come to know this over time, if you aren't aware of it already. A knife can last forever if you just act like it's your only one, and it's worthwhile, even rewarding to do so.

Efficiency and Safety

When the knife is in the forward position, the support hand should be floating somewhere in between your solar plexus and throat to provide a barrier to your vitals, and to create a safe place for your support hand to be.

By generally resolving never to use the support hand offensively unless immediately preceding or following a thrust or a cut to the outside (not crossing your body in a way that blocks your support hand) you can create reasonably safe conditions to use a fighting knife in. They will rotate; the empty hand falling back to guard the neck and the weapon hand falling back to full retention when they aren't striking.

Stand up and deliver a low elbow toward your six o'clock. If your hand is over your floating ribs, this is what I mean by full retention. From this position, it's most likely your support hand will be fully extended in the classic "stay back, buddy" position.

Now imagine those trading places. The weapon comes up from the midsection as the empty hand pulls back to the neck. Now the imaginary knife is extended fully in a thrust with the support hand guarding in the rear. They trade places again, knife dropping back to full retention as the empty hand strikes the face.

This is the standard response you will always be racing back to. A parry, cover, stop hit or suppress will open space for the ***Standard Response***. It is a design dependent technique: The blade must be in its most forward position, punch knives being the perfect example.

The edge must not face your support hand. Collision is a reality in solo training as well as in contact. If the framework for your training isn't safe, neither are your thumbs or radial artery.

Knife Application in Self-Defense

This is a mode of thinking more than anything, something I figured out during my training as an EMT. The medical community is filled with acronyms, my favorite being K.I.S.S. as in, *Keep It Simple, Stupid.*

S.A.S.C. will be your framework for knife application during drill.

Structural, Airway, Sensory, and Circulation. Each is a necessary part of a working body. Breaking the structure in an arm or leg would be severing a tendon. Maiming the limb would qualify as sensory if it puts the opponent into shock or circulatory damage if they bleed out. Airway should be obvious enough. The trachea, with the carotid arteries on each side, is your favored target regardless of what you are or aren't armed with.

This is all meaningless without an objective and your objective is largely based on context. As a civilian, your best bet is to evade after contact and let the police handle the rest. In order to evade, you have to make your opponent do something, such as fall down. S.A.S.C. should be used with the overall intent to destroy your opponent's balance. Drive back the weak points of balance—things shoulder and above, things hips and below.

The first key concept is ***take ground***. One ingredient cannot be done without any type of conflict. You must rapidly advance in order to win. Any free time your opponent has will hurt you. Give them no breathing space, no moving space, and no thinking space.

Two hands, one leg / inside entry is the name of the last dummy form in the Wing Chun lineage that I happen to be standing in. I see it as the perfect means of assessing risk with violent humans. If you engage the opponent head on, you risk coming in contact with two hands and one leg that could hit anywhere.

Outside entry is the only reasonable entry. If you happen to find yourself inside, in range of three weapons, fall back to the ***Standard Response***. Stomp forward and take ground, not stopping until the opponent falls over.

One can never truly know where the lethal strike in a string of three will land, on occasion, so just covering what you want to keep in ***compulsive cover*** is the smartest thing to do. Cover your face, throat and solar plexus; it's typically where the knife is going.

At the earliest point of convenience, retake ground and attack again.

In order to resist any force meaningfully, you'll need a low ***center of gravity***. In the knife context, however, you will need to balance that with mobility. You must be capable of moving in all directions and keep a consistently low center of gravity, preferably lower than your opponent's.

This comes with time and training; understanding how to

take on force is not something that can be done from the armchair.

The shortest distance between two points is almost always a straight line. Though I was shocked to see situations that made this premise false, it's still true nine times out of ten. If you slash at your opponent while he thrusts and you've both left your positions at the same time, he will hit first. If you both cut, you may need to reposition and reengage when you could have been escaping the scene.

Again, fall back on the ***Standard Response***: Take ground, thrust, hit, thrust until your opponent is grounded. This is economy of motion at its best.

Balance is weak in several parts of the body, so what you can do is create a ***disruption of balance*** in your opponent. "Where the head moves, the body follows" is a classic point to draw upon and it's this concept that is the most important part of the ***Standard Response.*** Balance is also weak in the lower aspects of the body. Cuts to the groin can cripple a low center of gravity, as will severing the tendons behind the knee or inner thigh.

The advanced application of the standard response should include a throw, reap, or severe damage to the knee. Any martial system can be applied to knife work. Wrestling may seem like the last thing you want to do, but gift wrapping an opponent or applying a double leg takedown applies the concept well enough.

You will discover what doesn't work in training. Eliminate the fallacies and all that remains is truth.

Knife Combat and the Sphere of Influence

This is an area of no recovery if you do not attack. The SOI is defined as the space you can affect without moving: arm's reach or weapon's reach. Once in contact at this range, you will not be able to outmaneuver your opponent, or see what techniques he may attempt.

Attack, attack, attack and continue moving forward. Once here, there is no Aikido, Karate, or even a bob and weave. Strike or be struck.

The ***Line in the Sand*** is one of choice and thought. It's the space you can affect after taking one big step. This big step—when taken by your opponent—gives you all the data you need to get outside (take the opponent's back) or even to catch the weapon hand in the case of the very skilled meeting the very unskilled.

Moving first and resetting the psychological dynamic of an altercation is the most important step. When someone moves aggressively toward you, they count on you not exceeding—let alone meeting—that energy.

Just taking little steps toward their back while they advance can be unnerving enough to end the confrontation there. Moving first can suppress weapons that aren't yet in play.

Consider two bodies moving in relation to each other. If a body turns to face and I move off-line, they must reset. Every time they reset, they need a new plan or at least to edit an old one. This is a confidence robber and gives you time to inflict a new tool or tactic to the situation.

If you can talk, do so. Forcing the enemy to think and respond to commands distracts from their ability to respond physically. Questions are ideal, but commands are realistic. Make your wishes known in the form of edicts: "Get back!" or "Make space, I'm leaving!"

Being on the receiving end will raise your heart rate and make you less useful. Replace his questions with your commands and never lose control of the conversation.

After you've spoken first, move first. Do as much as you can ethically first. Once a knife comes into play, being second and being dead is often the same thing.

It is important to remember ***high, low. Low, high.*** When the mind is bent on attacking a high target, it often becomes blind to those low targets. When someone tries to take your head off, they often forget that they leave their knees and groin completely open. (This has been touched on earlier, but we will expand upon it in this section.)

Should the opponent cut low and you have the space and time to articulate a wise move, cutting their face is likely the best choice. Things tend to collide in the low lines and your priority—in a standing altercation—will always be to hit the person before the weapon when possible.

When the opponent comes in high, cuts to the groin and femoral artery are your cheapest attacks. Greeting the force head-on is the most expensive. While both these choices can have terrifying outcomes attached to them, only one is guaranteed to leave you with severe lacerations.

The simplest way to understand ***outside and inside entries*** is to match them with the word *reach*. Inside entry implies that I am facing my opponent and that he can reach me with one of the previously mentioned three weapons available to a human at any given time.

Outside entry implies that he cannot reach me at all, that I have circled toward his back and am out of range of his weapons. Outside entry is easiest to attain from the ***Line in the Sand***—a place where you can calculate your opponent's movement to decide how he must attack.

Crawl Before You Sprint

Last and most important: take your training slowly. This exists to benefit you and your training partner. Injury will not benefit you, neither will death. Nothing can substitute expert instruction and quality sparring gear.

There is no legal advice here either, so crawling through your local law books could be a great next step. Lethal force isn't cut and dry. You are far more likely to use a blade against an unarmed group rather than a similarly armed opponent.

Consider that there's likely to be a large gap of time in which you haven't drawn your knife yet. Grappling occurs here, boxing occurs here. In order to apply your knife, you must first be competent in an unarmed skill set.

Think your training through carefully so that you can act quickly when it counts. Always seek a second opinion; doubt even this.

Part 3: Moy Yat Ving Tsun Journal

Do not leave home ahead of your sword and axe, for you cannot feel a fight in your bones or foresee a fight.

— The Hávamál

Chapter 15: A Focus on Training

This training journal was taken directly from Miles's iPad. Readers will notice similarity between what is discussed in the journal, and the subjects that have already been touched on earlier in the book. However, I have chosen to present Miles's journal as a separate section, rather than separating the entries and moving them into the previous sections, in order to preserve his voice.

December 22, 2012

Issues of trust and flexibility. Problems of communication and dedication. It's always been hard to find dedicated students and just as difficult to find a functional and trustworthy system. Making those two mesh has its issues. A person must be willing to empty their cup for their teacher in order to get anything done; it doesn't come naturally for most Americans, maybe most humans. It's hard for me to turn someone away when I find that their cup is full and impossible to tell someone to forget their preconceived notions—especially where life and death are concerned. Trusting a teacher means trusting your life to his judgment and leaving your preconceived notions freely.

Sifu means skilled, not master in the absolute. A cook can be a sifu, or a taxi driver: sifu of the taxis.

Anyone can teach if they are skilled, but what skill is best? Sau, Po, or Le? Bruce Lee was a sifu for sure, a creative force and a revolution for the martial arts community. However, he was all Le, all creativity and no system. He understood, but didn't transfer that system to his students properly (sorry, Jun Fan guys).

I believe I am Po. I have learned the system and I understand great swaths of it. Playing against a less experienced opponent, I can play creatively (Le) outside the system, sometimes without even accurately holding the center. But when the guy knows how to play too, I'm limited to the system. I have to play as I was taught because my Kung Fu just isn't that good yet.

So how much flex do I actually have? How much systemic tailoring can I do if I can't even play the system? I have to let it play me. When I do alter the system, I'm selling snake oil. I become a false prophet. I'm like Armor hot dogs: I get fat kids, skinny kids, and kids that play with rocks. They don't want to submit to the system and I'm not forcing them. They want it to change, become shorter, easier, and simpler.

Having the background I do, I know how simple it is to learn and how small it is comparatively. To someone accustomed to external rewards (goals, points, and accolades) the profit is less tangible. We have no ranking, no gold stars, just a polo if you're in the right place at the right time. Rewards are internal, subtle and sometimes the system itself is subtle; try making a Jut Sau work everywhere, or a Fook Sau. It's hard to mesh the system with the student when he is loaded up with his own ideas and you tell him, "This won't always work." He's here because he heard it was magic Kung Fu: make your own style Kung Fu, magic bullets and all that.

No system can house a mind like that. It would have to be big enough to fit the house he brought with him. Maybe that's the art in this martial system: learning to empty your cup, maybe that's all there is to it. All I know is I've been distracted and have to come back; I stink like snake oil, almost as bad as back in the days of my senior project.

December 23, 2012

Wing Chun is clearly a combat system, but it is steeped in and born of Chan Buddhism. It brings with it a culture and way of thinking that must not be abandoned. It makes the system work. Curiously enough, it invites two kinds of people: Zen practitioners and people concerned about their safety. Ironically enough, I hear more practical advice about fighting from the former, rather than the latter.

These are only two examples, but I can think of more. Wing Chun has been a reference for my knife carry and others have even applied it to football. It is a system, but not about one particular thing. When you learn this system and begin to apply it to your own ends, it is important to realize that all you actually understand is the system: not what you're looking at it through. No matter how hard I try, I'm not knife guy until I find a knife instructor; I'm still Wing Chun guy. I have no business teaching anything else until then.

December 26, 2012

Olsen is progressing. *[Miles was referring to a student he had been teaching at the time.]*

Nice to see hope come to fruition and to know, or at least believe my time isn't wasted. Currently, we are drilling basic strikes (high, low, low high) to the four corners: 12, 6, 3, and 9. Also, four basic elbow strikes, one legged Jong and Pak Sau and Tan Sau. I've only just introduced kicking. Since he still can't maintain on one leg, I know it's too early to have him try.

This is good, the basic picture of a quality fighting position:

able to hit in any direction, sufficient mastery of Pak Sau and Tan Sau and able to quickly raise a full defense of high, low, and middle. It's all pulled straight from the form, three from sections of Siu Nim Tau and the elbows from Biu Ji.

Going back to the previous entry about selling snake oil: Confidence is a trickster. I have my own priorities and concerns for personal carry and self-defense, and so I have my own way of teaching it. Not a big surprise, but it's hard to have confidence in something that only has your name on it. At least in the beginning, it's hard not to be anxious.

December 31, 2012

The system is more advanced than your understanding. A good system always will be, if not, it is likely incomplete. Committing yourself to a system is not a simple decision. Though the 'yes' or 'no' may be one word, it is a whole life that decides that answer. I am part of many lives—lives that will say yes or no based on my input and the input of others.

Should a man be storing gasoline to fight fire, it is my responsibility to tell them about my knowledge of fire, and that I don't think gasoline is the system he wants to be using. But, even in a situation as ridiculous as this, he still may know something I don't.

A good student of any craft—learning and applying his

system—must be ready to be wrong as well as passionate about being right. This balance separates amateurs from professionals, in every field from botany to religion. Rodents of men claim they are infallible, claim the logic of one man can apply perfectly to many.

Wing Chun is not perfect, no more than anything else. It is a system that best applies to stand up boxing, has little grappling and less ground application. But it is flexible and applying the system to the problems of combat tends to yield fruitful results, as I have with the knife.

It takes the principles of physics and turns them against the human body, through the human body. It is a system that relies on natural body positions and counter offensive strategy as opposed to clunky, defensive, offensive tactics. It applies well to pistols, knives, swords, sticks, and flashlights, but it takes understanding and a degree of mastery.

None of this works without an open mind, flexibility and total adoption of the systems you choose. Nothing will be found without total devotion, yet nothing still without open skepticism.

January 4, 2013

Guns have changed much and left much unchanged. As men, we stand between the past and future. How we pull these two together determines sanity, effectiveness and measures your heart. In Wing Chun, our Jong has one hand forward and one slightly behind, an extended hand and a half-retained hand. Today, I throw out half-retention where weapons are concerned.

Collision is embarrassing and potentially fatal and I don't see any major difference between knife and gun. In fact, they are so similar, it's possible to make a tactical error when you're trained to act differently with one or the other. The system they run under should be the same, as they are both short, concealable weapons.

I remember a certain martial artist, founder of the Drunken Wolverine style, I believe, fell into rough waters when he said some stupid things, one being a technique that espoused hiding the weapon with your lead hand.

A writer and martialist, Phil Elmore, pointed out that when any side of anything is weaponized, you clear it, you stay away; it's just common sense.

If you think you've drilled enough not to pin your hand to your opponent's chest, or not to make it into Swiss cheese with your favorite Glock, you, sir, are wrong. You will never out-train common sense, no more than you will ever out-earn your expenses.

Common sense must be a pillar of this club/system/style,

whatever it is or will become. Because of this, the knife will always be in full retention or fully in the lead, not behind the off-hand.

Also, I had a chance to train with Mr. Mertz today and we had a opportunity to play with Sifu Julio's cover and assault knife counter. It works like a charm, of course: it reminded me of how right Carl Cestari was about so many things, though not all, may he rest in peace. In spite of our many techniques in Wing Chun, they all do the same thing: They take the centerline. In spite of all its complexity, I often find myself in Tan Sau as my last resort. This is because it works and I don't know what's coming.

Don't worry about what the other person can or might do; only think about what *you* can do. I'll never forget that sequence. It changed the way I thought about martial arts forever. It moved it from a pursuit focused on the perfect defense, to one focused on awareness and acting quickly enough and correctly.

Common sense changed my life. Shame no one knew how to teach it.

January 6, 2013

Keep it simple, stupid. Very handy acronym. Never leave home without it. I was considering the ABCs of pre-hospital care (airway, breathing, and circulation) and promptly decided I need an equal. This isn't going to be perfect or pretty just yet, but here it is thus far. SASC: Structure, Airway, Sensory and Circulation. *(Note: This subject was discussed earlier in this text, as well.)*

If I damage your structure—sever a thumb or connective tissue in the knee or elbow—your effectiveness is greatly reduced. If I sever your airway, slash open an eye or open an artery, I have effectively neutralized you as a threat. Structure gives life to tactics, so it comes first. Airway gives energy to structure, so it is secondary. Without new information (sensory) you won't have a use for the airway or structure and of course, if you happen to be bleeding out, nothing will be very useful for long.

I tried to arrange these from highest percentage to lowest. Any changes are only natural; this is but a seed.

January 7, 2013

To be forced to fight the self is a terrible pity. To restrain a man who wishes to die is only natural, but to ask such a man to restrain himself is stupid; we aren't programmed for self-restraint. Still, I spent very little time doing what I do naturally. If I look back and stay honest, I've spent most of my life trying—mostly in vain—to reprogram myself.

Large problems manifest themselves in funny ways. Sometimes a stranger knows you better than you know yourself due to the incredible complexities of the human ego. So loathsome is this, it is often mistaken for the devil himself. If anything, it is the climax of unresolved issues that is the devil—small pockets of time so terrible, we only think of them in our dreams.

January 8, 2013

Freedom is a conceptual illusion. This country is built not on the ideal of freedom, but on the ideal of moving personal debt. Any breathing human being must acknowledge the fact of death, and so, understand that our freedom is relative. Still, among each other—inside this relativity—we are free.

Even I don't completely approve of the above paragraph, but I feel that it is accurate, at least in our modern era. The truth is elusive where our founding is concerned. What does freedom of religion mean when blasphemy laws stood with it? A thin tolerance was maintained by our Protestant forebears, and today, it is a full, almost unrelenting tolerance—at least among the non-believing.

What does the right to bear arms mean when magazines, velocity, and ballistics have changed so utterly? But maybe this is simpler, maybe this can be boiled down to a human's right to protect themselves and their property. Maybe, just maybe, religious freedom, too, simply means the right to call upon your Gods while understanding that you must respect the choices and emotions of others.

There's also a right of silence—not to incriminate oneself. This too comes with a silent clause: You must respect and love your government. To be silent in the face of justice when you have the power to bring truth is a sin. Perhaps freedom comes with responsibility and obligation. This, I feel, justifies the first paragraph. You are not free, not exactly, but still not a slave.

Living in a society where slavery is mostly abolished and entirely out of sight, I feel a tinge of guilt with what I am about to say, understanding that there are many here who wake up in hell with no hope of freedom and no understanding that only twenty feet away, there are people protected by a constitution and legally appointed representatives. I understand this. But as Americans in a Republic, definitions must change.

What is slavery in the land of the free? If I have trusted you to voice your opinion and have then attached the consequence of appointed representatives on the condition that you simply don't commit a felony, where does slavery come in? It comes in when I say I don't trust you anyway and tear the teeth from your mouth and the claws from your hands.

Some people say the Electoral College or gun registration is enough proof of mistrust. But anyone with half a brain knows there're plenty of people out there with less than that; we need a filter for ignorance and stupidity. I feel a new line coming in between us and our freedom, one that governs the just as though they were unjust and strips our freedom in anticipation of great evil.

When you do everything you can to help the system, submit yourself to its judgment and plug into its ideals, it hurts when it spits in your face, calls you evil, says it doesn't trust you. It hurts when it declares a separation of church and state, then tries to tell you how to govern yourself when you walk out of its sphere of influence. It's slavery in a modern sense, with prison at the fore, instead of a whip. It hurts.

January 11, 2013

I've trained Olsen in two techniques thus far.

1. Safety taking the centerline with an edged weapon and compensating with the empty hand.
2. Parrying an incoming weapon with the empty hand or weapon itself.

Now I find myself attempting to work Tan Sau and Biu Sau into the drills. This is not so simple, at least not on the face of it. We are still working with the rough product S.A.S.C. method. Structural, airway, sensory, and circulation.

With a sword or spear, a Tan or Biu takes the center and hits the vitals as quickly as possible. This is not practical with a carry knife as the weapon is still live, on the field and in range.

Considering the reaction of a cut body—it's about as bad as a cornered bear or lion. If you've moved the weapon and sever the airway or arteries, you have certainly killed your opponent, but you're probably about to head out yourself. Blinded, unable to take air or bleeding uncontrollably, the body will thrash, and with a weapon in a functional hand.

The parry (Pak Sau) is a bump: a forward moving technique that cuts another forward moving limb. This small interruption has huge results, sending the enemy weapon out of the center and opening an avenue of attack. With a knife, the same thing is done but with a cut at the end.

Tan Sau and Biu Sau applications differ in that they slash through material directly: edge facing forward, weapon hand moving forward, moving from bottom to top.

Project ruled temporarily unworkable.

Tan Sau and Biu Sau pushes weapon up, possibly up toward the face. Consider, train with it, and return later.

January 13, 2013

These ideas aren't terrible, just terribly limited. It's hard not to feel that there isn't any real power in a cut driven by a Tan Sau. It's also hard not to feel a little at risk the first time you cut a weapon hand with a Biu Sau. That said, it's still enough to remove a thumb or open an artery. All new things feel risky the first time you take them into the field. The only question that really haunts me as of now is this: Do we need this at all? The answer is probably yes.

January 14, 2013

I once heard of an idea called hydraulic decompression—tricking the mind into thinking a wound is much larger than it actually is, thereby producing more blood loss than would actually occur if the mind were able to process the information properly. Two little holes becoming one cannonball sized problem, according to your mind, anyway.

Whether or not this works is yet to be known, but the idea that one hit won't make him quit is far from new. Without significant damage to vital systems, your opponent will continue to function. I'll get right to the point.

Beginning in standard grip, you parry their weapon with your offhand, stepping to the outside. Then thrust your knife into the armpit, targeting connective tissue and perhaps the brachial artery, alternatively, you can also puncture the lung. Assuming he holds still, you will then remove your blade and come down on the mastoid process, carotid artery and trachea, bringing the knife up again into the throat/midline of his jaw. You will use this pressure to drive your target to the ground, remembering to control any remaining threats (empty hand and knife hand, elbows, legs, knees, etc.).

Order of events:
1. structural and circulatory; secondarily, airway and circulatory (lung puncture)
2. circulatory/airway
3. circulatory/control/sensory

I consider the last target sensory because you are *absolutely* controlling where he looks when you do this.

In reverse: parry, sever connective tissue (can't get a great lung thrust from this angle), come directly down into the subclavian artery behind the collarbone, control weapon hand and force body downward.

Order of events:
1. structural
2. circulatory

One could circle completely to the rear, but for legal reasons I can't advise assaulting a man from behind. Just giving you an idea of what's on my mind.

January 29, 2013

"I can do this. I do have something to offer." A rare thought in a field that has so much of what Han described as "sacrifice, denial, pain…" (If anyone remembers *Enter the Dragon*).

One of my greatest enemies is that I'm really not vetted by anyone. In spite of a decade of practice, I'm more of an EMT than a martialist. Go figure. But my model works, and I work; it's been witnessed and tested and I finally have enough material and testing of that material to really put together something good.

Chapter 16: The Holden Group

February 18, 2013

[Addressed to a student.] Here're five things we need to cover for your senior project. I'll be in tomorrow to run this if you have the time.

Positioning: High ground against low, standing against bended knee, bended knee against fallen. Always seek superior ground.

Controlling Range: This should be done verbally or all ground should be removed from the opponent physically. This carries with it the presumption that you have already tried to flee or have a legal right to be there.

Stepping to the Outside: Danger grows from the center and projects outward in order to protect the being. Circling toward the back negates both strength and weaponry.

Applied Jong: Looking at the horse, Jut Sau, and Wu Sau: These things are fine but they aren't non-combative. Trickery is the essence of good tactics and so it is best to go from passive to aggressive, that your enemy may not see your intentions.

Capturing the Centerline

To be *counter offensive* is not to hit first, but to come as close as possible to that ideal.

Acting First: A good way to act first is to speak first, to constantly circle to the outside and to look as though you are watching at all times. Better yet, to be watching at all times.

Taking Ground: I once heard an Indonesian say about combat, that the secret to winning is to always remember that he is standing in your spot. A sure way to sap your opponent's energy is to take his forward motion, to make him backpedal, to make him fall.

Aggressive defense is key to survival.

Imagine you don't know anyone and aren't accountable to any government. You are a stranger in this world; you don't know how you got here or where you're going. Defend your life in this way, with no fear and the belief that only you and what is familiar to you matters.

Forward is faster than backward.

Try it sometime. You often see people running drills forward and back as though their technique will actually stop someone from aggressively plowing forward. You cannot run backward, so don't even think of it.

Outside Entry: Since you cannot move backward, you must move forward intelligently. Go where he isn't moving and take your place back from him.

Flank, enter unguarded lines.

Always remember that only elbows can go backward effectively. Take gross advantage of this.

Destroying Balance: A knocked over opponent gives you space to escape or draw a weapon. Focus on shoulders up, knee down.

The head is sensory and without it the body cannot function. The neck delivers air and blood to that brain, and it can't function without that either. Hitting the groin isn't a terrible idea, but it's best not to bring your leg above his knee as it becomes easy to see and can corrupt your own balance. Hit to penetrate.

April 18, 2013

Everything else is style. These are the rules to aggressive self-defense, counter offensive Kung Fu. These are the functioning principles. How you apply it is your journey.

June 2, 2013

I've been training. Managed to recover up to form nine in

Shin Boep and hopefully up to twelve on Tuesday. My battle is internal. I am fortunate. It has renewed my ZaZen pursuits and I am hopeful for my sense of self in the future.

June 18, 2013

Martial arts can be problematic. They can give one the illusion they understand the situation when they only understand the content. Tyson is a great hitter, but when he was in prison they isolated him. He understands boxing, can hit hard and move swiftly, but he didn't understand the context of prison combat and was protected from it. In your little bubble of freedom, you will not be given that type of favor as you are the only one capable of granting it.

It is my intent to make hard hitters into efficient hitters. To know when, how, and where to strike based on context. That context is my own: civilian, in Pennsylvania, armed and with four limbs. How you act and react here is vastly different than in the ring or Dojang. This, however, shouldn't be taken as a slight against TMA: It will be our reference position, warm up, and the very material we draw from for combative solutions.

I will be splitting projects, neither removing myself from Dojang or Kwoon. It seems more in the interest of the general population to approach from context and how could I refuse when protecting day to day people is all it's truly good for anyway (excluding one's own well-being).

It is so that this will not be enough. It constantly vexes me that nothing is ever enough. You train with your weapons, body, and context (law, reality, and your own mental state) and any shortage leaves you feeling like you haven't done enough. But you will always come up short. Until the day you forget that there's a war out there, forget your weapons and leave your sanity—it will never be enough. So this, like anything else, is a place to start and a place to improve.

For now, we will be the Holden Group. We will drill empty hand, stick, knife, and flail. This requires the seeking out of many methods but only for the sake of solving one problem: close combat in Pennsylvania in twenty-thirteen. When I'm able, the pistol will make its way in as well. Anything that doesn't function will be ignored without apology. I am currently ready on every front but the gun: the drills are ready.

Front Toward Enemy: Wing Chun and Modern Close Combat

Dig In / Horse: The end result of a good stance should be shoulder width with knees bent. Like everything else, there is a margin of error and comfort involved. You may go further out, but know that you are actively trading movement for stability when you alter your stance.

Biu Sau method

This comes from beneath, thrusting into the centerline with an emphasis on the face (eyes and throat).

Siu Nim Tau Method

Front Toward Enemy / Facing: Always consider the weapon, the territory, and every other variable involved. What is good for you is not a constant.

Most Numerous Weapons

It's most logical to store what is vulnerable behind what is not. It is most logical to have more of one thing than another—little of the weak and much of the strong. When engaging, it is best to do so constantly with as little interruption as possible, targeting the weak instead of the strong.

Most Effective Weapon

With a long weapon, like a spear or rifle, the space that your weapon can affect makes all other tools irrelevant in the primary moments of contact. It is not to say that a shooter won't move laterally (right to left in relation to the target as opposed to closer or further) only that a more immediate concern can replace it, like shifting off-line to minimize your chances of being hit.

Take Ground / Taking the Center: This is inspired by *Hagakure* by Tsunetomo and Wilson. Consider how the hawk attacks—slightly off-line, fully committed, employing claws, beak and body weight. Consider the last form in the dummy—two hands, one leg. Attack fully committed with all the tools you can employ and constantly take ground.

June 28, 2013

How do you cover your ass in the modern civil battleground? Where I am, the law and culture is permissive and I am left with three simple things: Learn, Train, and Arm. It is a circle, training with new tactics and weapons, learning of new methods and tools and arming yourself with the best you can make available. If you aren't strong, you will die. If you aren't smart, you will die, and if you reject what is logical, you will die.

June 30, 2013

Nature of Material: Context based Wing Chun; personal concerns

Nature of Student: Mature adult

Weak Spots: Dexterity, flexibility, lack of immersion

Before all else, a man must be flexible and familiar with his own body, its limits and attributes. My experience in Shim

Gum Do will rectify that.

Next is dexterity. Pak Sau, Tan Sau, Gan Sau, Gum Sau, and Chi Gurk must be drilled heavily and with great intensity.

Immersion is difficult, and this is what separates the initiated from the obsessed by degrees. A good student immerses themselves first, but a good teacher does exactly the opposite—first training the virtues, before giving the student over to the oceans of information.

You must insist on clean transmission; this is a laboratory, after all.

Next day

[Miles is discussing a student.]

Before everything else, I must improve his consistency in the guard. I've accepted Full Guard as our first Basic, a mixture of Tan Saus and Tan Gurks—lateral and medial—with squats in between each 'presentation.' Then we will drill Tan Sau more, finally Tan Dar and close with whatever he wants.

1. Stretching. 10 minutes.
2. Full Guard and Pressing the Enemy (crucifix pushups, diamond and standard). Maybe 15 minutes.
3. Tan Sau. 15 minutes.

4. Tan Dar. 15 minutes.
5. Tan Gurk. 15 minutes.
6. Closing. 20 minutes.

An hour and a half, best guess.

July 4, 2013

I am coming closer to freedom everyday. Someday I intend to return to the Shim Gwang Sa and continue my ZaZen training.

Chapter 17: Final Thoughts

Aug 16, 2013

Positivity is not one of my natural proclivities, but things are looking up. A new job is within striking distance, my con-ed is nearly complete and I will soon return to my Wing Chun pursuits. My rage at injustice has only found more targets, regretfully. Things I used to take solace in, I now resent, and this is unfortunate but it's still positive change. Humanity is constantly realizing it has been tricked and learning from this trickery is natural. This is positive.

Aug 16, 2013

I will not teach anyone who will not adhere to the system, for I am ignorant without it.

I will come closer to the Moy Yat family for I cannot improve without them.

I will focus on the art over the application because life is more than death.

I will be cautious in who I trust with the system and will not follow my emotions but my interest.

Aug 16, 2013

Three factors form the unified theory. This will change, but for the moment they are Surprise, Timing, and Response. Having a well-articulated response separates the efficient from the time wasters: This is the key between taking one attacker or three. Getting the most out of your weapon system is the point of this theory or formula.

Surprise

Facing is natural and inevitable. Several attributes must be added, however, before surprise can become beneficial. Like a rock climber, you must hold on. You must be more determined, stronger in stance and intent. Digging in is as simple as lowering your center of gravity, preferably lower than your enemy's, but since you don't know him, just do your best.

The right stance should come from experimentation, not just someone who claims qualifications and promises something will function properly. Some stances are strong against lateral force, some against medial force. Finding what works well for both is best all around.

Also, think about how you can deliver the most force. Don't trick yourself into thinking you will be able to shift stances in a way that favors your skill set: train realistically and with realistic variations.

Timing

This is relatively simple; generally speaking it takes around a quarter of a second to see, decide, and respond if you have a basic idea of what you're involved in. Learning from qualified instructors and experience tells you what you can do. Training with that information and experience boosts confidence and shortens your response time. It's possible to see and respond in a tenth of a second. It is also safe for those who may be concerned about using unjust force. There's only one way to act violently, only one way to invade someone's space. Trust that you can recognize it, learn more about it, and have faith in yourself.

To act with a sense of order, we need to make general assumptions: that your enemy is going to take your head off and not slap your bicep, and that there are certain areas and methods that must be protected and espoused. Dropping your jaw down will protect your trachea, moving your elbow into your center protects whatever is still exposed of your neck, to just below your solar plexus.

Now that you've protected your high priority areas, we can address the possibility that the attacker isn't headed for those particular targets. Low blocks and leg techniques are important, but not as important as removing the opponent's ability to strike. Once you've recognized violent behavior inside your personal space and acted to protect yourself, it then becomes important to take the fight to the enemy.

Response

I'd like to address how, but that's a little more difficult and time consuming. The truth is, it takes years to become truly competent at striking; thought, knuckle pushups, bag work, and cardio will come into play somewhere. Where and why is what we will focus on here.

Let's start with the last place you want to go: the core. There's too much muscle and general density for this to be a "go to" target, not to mention the fact that it happens to be the most natural point to defend. This is the place you're going to skip in a best case scenario.

If all goes as planned, you will go from the face and neck to the groin, to the knees and repeat. This method disrupts the center of gravity to such a degree that you can ground a target instead of having to beat them unconscious. This gives you space and time to draw a weapon and retreat.

Conclusion

This is my litmus test for any martial system. If I don't see this in action, they don't see my money. If you can extrapolate this from a given method, fantastic. Earnestly test it and if you find that it doesn't add up and you can do better, then find better. Your life depends on it.

Martial arts are like religions. They provide comfort, utility, and an impressive culture. But not all provide utility the way they should and in no way should you shortchange yourself on truth.

Chapter 18: Wing Chun Personal Interview

Toward the end of 2011, Josh Mertz met Miles. Around November of 2012, he began compiling information for his high school senior project on martial arts and Wing Chun. While he worked on his project, Miles and Josh met three days a week and practiced for an hour or two. Along with Wing Chun, Miles also taught him combat training, and showed him how to fight and disarm attackers with weapons. Josh graduated from Tinicum Art and Science in 2013. This personal interview with Miles was part of Josh's project, included here with his permission.

Josh: What got you started in Wing Chun?

Miles: I wanted to complete my understanding of combat boxing. I still haven't, but WC is a big part of that process. I found it by chance, was very fortunate and blessed to have such good timing. With my devotion to Zen martial arts, I have been given two distinct perceptions that continue to fuel my interest.

J: When did you first start Wing Chun?

M: I found one of [my] Sifus' flyers in my work. He happened to want to start teaching out of his house. It may have been mid-2011.

J: Have you had to defend yourself in a real life situation using Wing Chun?

M: I've used the principles in a few altercations, but never have been in any serious situations since. I'm too old to get in trouble.

J: When do you practice?

M: Sometimes I lose faith and I don't play the system, but every day I'm doing something. I do the forms probably in excess of two times a day. I play with the ideas constantly.

J: Do you practice every day?

M: Yes. When you take this on, you're attempting to alter your unconscious responses. It takes years, so hurry.

J: Do you practice in one area or do you like different environments?

M: I play with the environment a lot. I do deeply believe that the ground can kill you as quickly as your opponent. Being familiar with the ground—its gentle rises and steep drops—can often be a defining feature of victory or defeat.

J: Do you have anyone who you look up to?

M: Colin Powell. The first non-fiction I ever read was his biography. The Powell Doctrine is exemplified in Wing Chun and he is too far away for my respect to be tarnished or my hero worship to fade.

J: Why do you like Wing Chun?

M: WC is science and with Chi Sau there is no false Kung Fu. It cooks or it leaves the kitchen. Also, the Zen aspects have their own daily benefits.

J: Do you think it's important for everyone to know?

M: Yes. It's silly not to take responsibility for your own health and self-protection. It's a simple, short form and the principles apply well to the pistol and knife. Very modern, very compact.

J: Do you plan to continue with this as long as you can?

M: As long as humanly possible. Its been a wonderful social/cultural experience and it's a beautiful thing to bring to patient people.

J: Any martial art besides Wing Chun that interests you?

M: Thai boxing, Systema, Krav, Catch as Catch Can wrestling. I've also considered taking some time off to study

Western medieval martial arts, mediaeval combative systems, which consists of armed, unarmed, armored, and unarmored, mostly sword fighting. I'd love to try anything.

J: If so, do you find one better than the other?

M: A well-oiled handgun is the best Kung Fu.

J: Do you plan to pursue anything involving Wing Chun?

M: I'd like to have a small group. I intend to force the time into being this year and really form a small tight training circle. We shall see how successful I am.

Part 4: Memories and Miles's Personal Sphere of Influence

All the entrances, before you walk forward, you should look at, you should spy out; for you can't know for certain where enemies are sitting, ahead in the hall

— Gestaþáttr, Hávamál, a poem found in the Codex Regius, Old Norse poems.

Friends, family, teachers, and students were asked the question:

How did Miles affect your life?

This simple inquiry opened many doorways.

Each of the following chapters delves into how Miles changed the lives of others, by caring for those he loved, sharing knowledge, and being willing to continuously learn.

The sphere of influence is that which one person—or one body of energy—can affect within reach of their centerline.

Miles's sphere of influence extended much further than he ever imagined.

Chapter 19: Sneak Attack

Rosa Sophia

Miles and I were angry children, and we took it out on each other. As kids, he beat me up, but as teenagers at Tinicum Art and Science high school, he would sneak up behind me, put me in a choke hold with my own hair, and say, "See? You need to learn to defend yourself or someone is going to kill you one day." He wanted to protect me. We loved each other, but we didn't know *how* to love each other.

At Tinicum, Miles frequently orchestrated sneak attacks on me, in between classes. Stephanie, our math teacher—who became like a surrogate mother to Miles—walked out of a classroom holding a mug of tea and shaking her head, laughing, one hand on her hip. I gripped Miles's arm, trying to push him off me, while Stephanie said, "Oh, you Holden kids. Look at them. Aren't they cute?"

Other teachers laughed, and students giggled.

"Yeah, real cute," I grumbled while Miles's arm pressed against my trachea.

Finally, he would let me go, but not before giving me a lecture about watching my back, because I was clearly unprepared for unexpected combat. The sneak attacks continued. Miles said I needed to be on guard at all times, prepared for the unforeseen. He gave me lessons in self-defense despite my constant insistence that I would never need such knowledge. Looking back, I now realize a lot happened to Miles that he didn't talk about. He went through hell, and kept it to himself. We have a lot in common that way—a tendency to repress. Our father was quiet, as well, and perhaps we both inherited that from him.

Miles believed in being prepared. But I think we both struggled with deep-seated fears. And, as someone who has been hurt too many times to count, I can't blame him.

* * *

While he was still in public school, as a child, Miles got in trouble for drawing ninjas in class. The teachers felt he was exhibiting tendencies toward violence, and our mother argued he was just expressing himself creatively. Neither of us fit in when it came to public school. Miles went through a few alternative schools before finding Tinicum Art and Science.

After that, I joined him there, and it was the best thing that happened to both of us.

There, Miles was able to dig into his love of martial arts. He studied Shim Gum Do, and traveled to the Dojo in Boston. He wanted to move to Boston, and I heard him say on more than one occasion that he *would* live there one day. It was just a matter of time.

I worried about him when I moved to Florida. I often considered moving back to Pennsylvania just to look after him, to protect him. From what, I didn't know.

During one of my visits, his car had died in the parking lot at his old job, and he didn't have jumper cables. I took him to Walmart and bought him a set, then showed him how to use them. I showed him how to check the belts and hoses, and explained monitoring the fluids in the car. On more than one occasion, he called me while I was in Florida because he was having car problems.

People would say, "How's your brother doing?"

"I don't know," I would say. "He only calls me when he's having problems with his car."

As we grew older, we became close friends. Miles would threaten to kill any man who tried to hurt me—while twirling a knife in his hand, of course.

The second time I moved to Florida, he came with me for

a vacation. That was the last time we were together. He seemed okay—not great, but okay. One night, he drank too much and sobbed, letting out the sorrow that he always denied while sober. I held him while he wept, told him everything would be okay. I even offered to help him find a place to live and a job if he decided to move south. I would've done anything for him.

One day, our old friend Braden Kirkpatrick rode his bike to my house from Stuart, where he'd been living in the woods after riding his bicycle all the way down from Pennsylvania. I told Braden he looked like Tom Hanks from *Castaway*, and Miles grinned and lit another cigarette. That day, the three of us spent time with my mother, who was also visiting. We'd been together so much in high school that it felt strange, all of us in the same place again, only we were twelve hundred miles from our old house in Telford that had since been condemned.

While Miles and Braden walked down the sandy road away from the house, headed for the convenience store down the street, I took a photo of them as they walked and laughed, their backs to the camera. I looked at my mother and said, "This is just amazing that we're all here today. How strange! They're going to want this picture one day."

That was the first week of May, 2015. In August of that

summer, Miles committed suicide. He once stood in my living room practicing his forms, which he did every single day. His entire focus always remained on his training.

What I wouldn't give to watch him do that—just one more time—his arms extended before him, his body moving as if dictated by a choreographed dance, his mind focused on everything around him.

Prepared.

Ready.

Expecting the unexpected.

Chapter 20: My Nephew

Brenda Godshall Haberle

The first clear memory I have of Miles is when I saw him, and Rosa, riding bikes on the baseball field near their house next to Branch Creek when they were around six and nine. Before that, I can recall being at their dad's house and Miles and Rosa were running around as toddlers. That day, when I saw them on their bicycles, I wanted to talk to them. I had "stalked" that place for a while, hoping I would someday see them out playing and introduce myself, which is what I did that day. I walked up to them.

"You two don't know me," I said, "but your dad is my brother."

Neither of them knew what to say, and the feeling was awkward. I'll never forget the look on Miles's face. He was so skeptical about this person who said she was his aunt.

Unfortunately, I did not see him again until he was a young adult.

I remember him sitting at my mom and dad's house, his grandparents. Funny, at first I thought he was a little strange, but the more I listened to him talk, the more I realized he was just a very deep thinker.

As much as he liked to talk, he seemed to listen even more, taking in what others had to say and processing it. I had a good time with him when we went to the bay in Maryland in 2014. He seemed like he had not been on a vacation in a long time and was just taking it all in.

I wish I had gotten to know him more. He left us way too early.

Chapter 21: Childhood Friends

Morgan Rank

Growing up, I'm pretty sure I spent endless amounts of time either at Miles's house or him at mine. At school we were usually always together. He loved the outdoors, action movies, knives—he always had one—and so much more.

I remember so many different things we did together and with his sister; it was as if we were family. We spent time at the tennis courts by the house, the creek, and just went about being children.

I left Miles's life when he switched schools. But when my mom would drive by, I'd always look to see if I could see him, or think about the times we had playing together.

Miles was just so simply beautiful in every way that only the people who walked with him would understand him and just how beautiful he was, how he touched people and their hearts without having to try.

He will be forever missed and I'm proud to have walked with Miles awhile down his path.

Chapter 22: My Son Miles's World Map

Ruby Lynn Holden

I miss the early evening chats with my son Miles in our living room, where we sat in comfortable mission-style wooden chairs, a chess table between us. On the wall at that end of the room was a large laminated map of the world; it often influenced the course of our conversations.

On a particular evening I recall, we were discussing world politics. I voiced the opinion that the map featuring the Americas at its center should rather have Europe and Africa as its visual center.

In a flash, Miles stood, drew a knife from his pocket and slashed the map vertically into four sections. I retrieved the staple gun from a kitchen drawer and we rearranged the sections.

Miles was a radical and deep thinker, for which I take some

credit. I always encouraged Rosa and Miles to think critically, to question everything, to regard the emperor's new clothes with skepticism. But I am so thankful for the education they both received at Tinicum Art and Science, so grateful to their teachers, the Best of the Best.

Through the years, I observed Miles's dedication to his martial arts practice. More recently, it has inspired me to achieve greater strength of body and mind through my deepened yoga and my own martial arts practice.

Chapter 23: Always In Motion

James Lysoby

Suicide has taken another life way too soon.

Miles, I still remember meeting you in my early days of working at the deli. I can't remember how many ice cream cones I scooped for you and your sister, but it was a lot. When you were a kid, your biggest concerns back then appeared to be what ice cream flavor to choose, and what new ways you could find to tease your sister.

Really, so many memories I have of you involve food, whether it was you ordering a veggie melt on the "least skanky bread possible" or you taking home an entire box of day-old donuts and downing them in one sitting.

The years went by and you certainly grew up a lot. I remember helping to get you the Christmas tree job and the smile on your face every time you got a big tip. I also remember the time a stray cat starting hanging around the lot and you took him home and named him Mr. Kennedy, after the wrestler.

Everything you did was unique. You had a style and a way that was all your own, one I could never fully put into words. You were a great guy, even if you didn't always realize that.

As time passed and I watched you grow up, I realized that you were one of the deepest thinkers I had ever met. Your mind was always in motion. You always sought knowledge and truth and could debate anyone about any subject. There were so many thoughts in your brain and a lot of them were quite profound. I wouldn't always agree with you, but I couldn't help but see certain things in a different light after even a few minutes of speaking with you.

You will be missed more than you know.

Chapter 24: "Why so serious?"

Stephanie Kenney

Thinking flexibly, being proactive, and staying optimistic are sometimes your only assets; never leave them at home.
— M. D. Holden

I met Miles about ten years ago when he came into my math class at Tinicum Art and Science. He was typical of the kind of student we had back then—clever and bright but somewhat lazy and disorganized. Disenchanted with school and large organizations in general. What was different about Miles was his constant wit, sharp and sudden, and his relentless questioning practice.

We connected around martial arts, Japanese, and philosophy. He was like a sponge absorbing and remembering everything I said, examining it all at his leisure, and returning to me with his insight and depth and more questions. This suited my philosophical bent and many long and complicated conversations ensued.

When Miles graduated, we kept in touch. Sometimes speaking several times in a week and sometimes not for months. He would go out and experiment in ways of living and come back to sit and analyze his choices with me. We talked through relationships, employment prospects, religious conviction, politics—you name it. He had dinner at my house and with my family. My son Emmett adored him. We spent holidays together. He was family.

I am not sure I ever met anyone who was trying harder to live a truly authentic and principled life. Our relationship demanded a very committed kind of honesty and trust and it was an honor to both give and receive. And boy, did he make me laugh!

These are a just a few text exchanges with Miles that show what I mean.

Jul 30, 2014

Miles: Hey tiny, do you know if Tinicum files form 990 for a charitable non-profit?

Stephanie: I am sure we do, you could check with Tina. Why?

Miles: That's tempting but I'm on the clock. I see. Sucks to have a dog in the fight on the side you want dead.

Stephanie: Hmmm.

Miles: The FFRF is suing the federal gov for supporting an unconstitutional law from the fifties … its going to affect religious institutions and charities … if it ever flies.

Stephanie: [Name removed] like?

Miles: Those fuck nuts are a whole other issue. *[Miles was speaking of a business. The name of the business has been removed.]* It's just about tax exempt status and declaring monies, which is currently voluntary for religious organizations but mandatory for charities. Trying to level the playing field. And on that note … having a bunch of Catholics vote against a bunch of women on a female's issue is bullshit.

Stephanie: Not just female issues. It's a big question especially with big corporations.

Miles: It's true … but i can't win with that. That's something idiots call a sacrifice. If i make it look like you're kicking a puppy I'll turn a whole crowd of fence sitters on my side … not that ladies are puppies in any way.

Stephanie: Lol!!!

Miles: Here it is in English: You can't reason someone out of something they didn't reason themselves into. You can bet the farm that shame is one of the main reasons for unjustified belief. Refocus that shame and change the belief. It's like talking to fucking rocks frankly, but you gotta make the rockslide go your way. I'm growing something great ... something new.

Aug 1, 2014

6:47:44 AM, Miles: You up yet?

8:32:16 AM, Miles: Perhaps now?

8:34:35 AM, Stephanie: Oh good morning Miles. Are you on the way?

Miles: I could be ... once i put on shoes.

Stephanie: Ok see you soonish

Miles: Indeed

Stephanie: Indeed. Its lovely out!

2:07:27 PM, Miles: That was some damn fine rhetoric earlier.

Stephanie: Very fun, albeit too early for me to get fully in stride. You have a gift. Well many actually.

Miles: If you were in full stride id open a damn whole foods pharmacy.

Aug 31, 2014

Miles: Hey, when you've got the time, could you crack my Peco and send me the account number? And perhaps the amount i owe. It seems a little like asking someone to fold your underwear ... but i am quite far from the laundry.

Stephanie: I will do it tomorrow

Nov 28, 2014

Miles: it appears my car will be done today. can i see you soon?

Stephanie: Out and about in D-town today and Nutcracker in Philly tomorrow. What are your plans Sunday or Monday?

Miles: i could come up Sunday.

Stephanie: Ok let's touch base Sunday morning.

Miles: thank you.

Stephanie: Thank you

Miles: sorry. im doing my panicky thing

Stephanie: Hope it eases :)

Miles: I'll let you know either way. i hope your weekend's ballin out of control

Stephanie: Hmm got puked on in the middle of the night ... little sleep. Hope tomorrow's ballet is more fun. Stay warm.

Miles: Yowza ... i forgot the price of that homie feeling in life. Ha-ha!

Dec 31, 2014

11:38:53 PM, Miles: i love you in a nonuniversalist, totally concrete way! happy impending new year!

Stephanie: Love you too!! HNY hope it is your best year yet

Feb 16, 2015

Stephanie: Hey where you at? Did you fall off the map?

Miles: still on the map. resolved some key issues and have been having loads of sex as a result ... and the snow keeps me down. how are you?

Stephanie: Dealing with frozen and burst pipes but otherwise warm and toasty. Glad you are well

Miles: ah the perils of the home owner ... if a younger Stephie had her way, that would have been redistributed by now.

Stephanie: It's busy that's for sure! Hey do you want me to forward mail to your new address. You may have some important things in there

Miles: true ... it seems like getting down is harder than i expected ... didnt factor snow or sex

Stephanie: Winters should have lots of both

Miles: that's a fantastic response

Stephanie: Well ... Just keeping it real. So if you give me an address I'll try to get it done in the next few days

Miles: right! ... Orthodox Street, Phila 19124

Stephanie: Funny, I think of you as unorthodox

Miles: they wouldn't take me!

Mar 22, 2015

Miles: Why so serious? *[Texted image of Miles wearing a clown nose, a gift from Stephanie.]*

Stephanie: Uh-oh, emergency clown [nose]? Emmett needed that earlier today too. How are you?

Miles: Having a pretty good day … though i have this really irritating urge to leave the east coast. spring has sprung … so has my annual get shit done madness. what could such a young person need a clown nose for? *[Speaking of Emmett.]*

Stephanie: The tragedy in young man's life knows no bounds. I think leaving the east coast is not a terrible idea. Where do you want to go?

Miles: i want to see the desert. new mountains. the smartest people i know are doomed to being downtrodden and im tired of putting on the white gloves for the people i care about. They're supposed to be adults. this pond is too small

Stephanie: Yep. Don't wait!

Jun 9, 2015

Miles: Loved human!

Stephanie: Hey Miles! Guess what I'm doing?

Miles: You are … balancing out a five year plan … making next year's class schedule or wrestling a small bear over a small tin of soup. Back in my old hood again? I really miss being able to find quiet places to train outside. The city blows if your not publically intoxicated.

Stephanie: I don't recommend that. Come for a visit?

Miles: I shall. How does your Saturday go?

Stephanie: Looks pretty clear :)

Miles: I will come down.

Jul 26, 2015

Stephanie: What's happening Miles?

Miles: Not much. Mostly just arguing with creationists, hanging out with Joëlle. You?

Stephanie: Just one of those summer relax weeks. Enjoying. Just checking in

Miles: How's business?

Stephanie: It's going. I am psyched to do Musikfest. Hope it's a good fit. No plots just checking in ... and worrying about you a little :)

Miles: I'll make it. Just have to get out of here. Never did catch Musikfest. Heard one year a couple angry moms shut down a mosh pit. Probably pretty safe if they have that kind of veto power

Stephanie: That sounds funny

Miles: I wish I could make myself laugh. I seem to have a

knack for funny these days. Had a good time?

Stephanie: Had some folks for dinner. I had fun. How is Joëlle?

Miles: She's fine. Just trying to find a way out of marketing cheese ... retail can really get you stuck sadly

Stephanie: I bet you cheer her up. She seems solid. You do need to get out of here. Are you able to put any aside to travel?

Miles: I might have a better way out. Cooking it now, I'll know more next month. Hard to tell who's doing the cheering. I suppose it could explain why she puts up with me.

Stephanie: Puts up with you? You are a fun, entertaining, and very good friend, Miles. Good luck with your plan. Goodnight.

Miles: Goodnight.

As for exits, there are two kinds: exits in known areas and exits in unknown areas. In a place you know, you have choices. You can weigh them out in a split second and be through the door immediately. In a place you don't know, there is only one safe exit; once the engagement has begun and you can no longer look around, it is only behind your opponent.

— M. D. Holden

Chapter 25: Teacher Meets Student

Julio Ojeda

I was teaching Wing Chun at my house, and I taught and trained Miles for about eighteen months. Miles had found a flier I left at the grocery store where he worked, and the first time I met him was in an interview I set up in 2011. I don't just take any student. I first talk to them to see why they want to learn the art.

Miles was different than other students; all he wanted to do was learn about weapons and how to use them in martial arts. I explained that I couldn't teach weapons without going through the process of learning the system first, and he agreed.

I have two sons who don't want to learn anything about the art. From there, Miles became more than a student; he was like a son to me.

Back in the old days, Wing Chun was meant to be a kept secret, divulged only to one's trusted family members.

He ate at my house every day that he came to train, to the point that my mother-in-law had his food ready as soon as we finished training.

After he passed the last form—Biu Jee—to become an instructor, I gave him a wooden dummy as a gift. Miles loved that thing more than anything.

He was so happy. I still remember it like it was yesterday.

Sometimes we didn't train at all, we just sat and talked about life, work, April—his girlfriend at the time—my country of Puerto Rico, and many things.

Miles will be missed for sure.

For some reason, I think he would still be here if he had come and sat with me and talked ... who knows.

Chapter 26: Letter to Miles

A Poem by Peter Ryan Sabom Nim

I am sorry to have missed you.

Sometimes a person has to get up and go, and that i understand.

It really isn't my nature to do so, but to be honest i have considered it.

A kind of ballast accumulates with family and a school and a community, which makes for steadiness but transforms one into a cargo ship of the North Atlantic, all heavy seas, slow turns, and big picture.

So I remain in Riegelsville,

for every intent and nearly all purposes a sycamore tree.

I contemplate the sky and people know exactly where to find me. Here, too, is an apology for not writing sooner.

We saw each other so infrequently, especially in light of

how fond i am of you,

some part of me doesn't quite register that you left.

I mean, i have a neighbor who might be on vacation and i wouldn't know.

It might take half a year, if the sidewalk was being shoveled and the grass cut,

for their absence to sink in.

So there is something, maybe dreamt of years ago,

that expects you to shimmer over to school, draped with a sardonic and philosophical turn of mind,

and, in diffidence, hold court in my chambers.

This is something i always enjoyed from you, though the distance you kept left me uneasy.

I had some of the same a few decades ago.

Friends found me confusing, especially friends who wanted to be much, much closer.

"When he is serious, he is joking; when he is laughing, he is deadly serious"

is how someone who actually stood fast by me gave as a heads up to an aspiring intimate.

I sense that you provide a similar confusion to those who love you.

It is a gift, i think, to others, at times.

Maybe, as your youth wanders off somewhere,

you will become comfortable with what is left to you.

It is an inheritance, you will soon know, from your prior self. Maybe undeserving, maybe unwanted, and certainly freighted with unwieldy stuff.

But there it all is,

a dowager passing on obscure drawings, rare coins,

and stale air to the family rebel.

Sell what you can and leave.

I heard, from someone i don't know but who knows you,

that you are in Shakespeare, New Mexico.

A ghost town.

The only American town named after a writer.

It is hard to make a living in a ghost town,

but easy to make a ghost out of a writer. All that abstraction and loneliness.

The drinking, the sage brush, the creaking movie sets.

Good luck to you, with all that, Miles.

I won't pass on any personal news, as things are moving very swiftly and under their own locomotion.

I think ghosts and trees have an altogether different sense of time than other sorts of beings.

A squirrel is an itch, a blur to a tree.

God only knows what a person is.

And ghosts, what can be said about ghosts?

I recall being warned by my doctor to never sleep under open windows in Yunnan.

He said the region is a thicket of hungry ghosts,

mouths agape, wanting wanting wanting, everything they never had.

It is easy to pick up and move for some people.

I think ghosts have a curse on them—it is too easy to move on. Which is why they get so stuck in returning.

They are a bit like mollusks, a pillow of flesh,

seizing onto what ever they can.

I suppose the reason i am writing you has something to do with my feeling that i let you down.

Not that i feel badly about it.

I don't think me, then, could have done differently.

I entered that hell you and your friends were in and drew you out towards our school.

This was years ago, a decade ago.

To be perfectly frank, i was exhausted and choked with sadness. It is very straightforward for me to evoke that moment of intense sobbing,

of relief and abject fear, and let it go.

But still it sprawls there, a swamp.

Something dankly human, but lost to my understanding.

It sort of gathers itself up, with dull politeness and unacknowledged agitation,

looking blankly at me and turning away.

There is about you something of a snail, don't you think?

Even in the easiest conversation, a mild gesture might stamp on you, and you'd withdraw for a week.

Catherine Spurgeon, in my very favorite book of literary analysis, illustrates Shakespeare's unerring sympathy for the victim of any harm:

> *[the] snail, who tender horns being hit,*
> *Shrinks backward in his shelly cave with pain,*
> *and there all smother'd up in shade doth sit,*
> *Long after fearing to creep forth again...*

I felt from you that tentative reach every so often; i know i often missed so much.

Its a rabbit hole to speculate on why a person develops as they do. I don't recognize myself sometimes.

When we met, early in the life of the school,

and there was that intimidating chaos swirling around you;

i can say from this late perspective that i wasn't ready to help. Too many institutions and people had let all of us down,

so i didn't trust what was out there. In a sense, we all were adrift.

But we tried to make something new, a different sort of school, something a strange bird could nest in for a while.

Maybe it worked, maybe it didn't.

I wanted you to find a home, for you to attach to something,

for the storm to quiet down,

that you might sense the more fleeting,

surer movements within yourself.

Miles, but i see how you act,

and it seems to me you can't reconcile your mistrust of others with your longing for things to be fixed and permanent.

Anybody who appears and disappears as you do is a ghost and a barnacle,

and leaves the rest of us hoping and wondering. And worrying.

But that independence of yours cuts both ways, too.

It is as if you have faith and doubt completely inverted.

Doubt is a sword, a tool. It comes from the head.

It is critical, skeptical. But it is not a ground to push off from.

Faith is that ground, in the guts.

It is where the most powerful movement comes from,

as even a beginning martial arts person knows.

Doubt in the guts is poison; faith in the head is blind.

And you radiate doubt. At least you used to.

And then, there are your beautiful public demonstrations of faith. Such as when you spent weeks and weeks teaching a young man at our school.

I think you saved his life. He was dedicated to you, animated by you.

I don't quite comprehend how you, Miles, in some kind of suspended, acrobatic

moment, could push off your own floating self and transform this kid.

I can see your own roots drifting above the ground, never taking hold, even gathering

up into itself. But there was sense, too, that you longed for the ground,

that you wanted to meet it, penetrate it, to hit it very, very hard.

To feel real. To wake up.

But all of the sudden, now thoroughly mixing up the metaphors, you retracted right back into your shell.

You doubted, and fled. You didn't abide.

I am unsure of how i missed you.

When you were practicing at the school, you had a dedication and intensity far beyond

my own.

My teaching was immature, scattered.

You sought out greater teachers, which was wise. You found them. That was fortunate.

I am a slow learner; i seem to take things in spaciously, in great amounts, and slowly find the depths and get taken with the surface play of light, shapes, spectres.

You seemed to plunge right into it, into the ghosts, the depths.

Which is why, when you moved, i sent you that Chan text that Christine and i translated.

It seemed to capture something about you, something both dark and light:

> *On a towering peak*
> *Unknown by demons and outsiders;*
> *In the deepest sea walking,*

remote from spying buddhas.

With dark and light, too, we can go back to that sense of attachment, and to doubt and faith.

How attachment has this yin and yang quality,

of attachment, its western sense, being committed, being dedicated, of being unconditional,

of being protected early on in life,

of finding loyal, honest friends,

and finally, lovers and partners in great works.

It is a very yang sort of thing;

but it also has a deeply yin quality as well, of receiving, accepting, abiding.

But, again, in that eastern sense, it is emptiness,

the empty sky, there is no center, no beginning or end, and spaciousness for all beings.

And here we are, thinking "oh, attachment!"

and i have a feeling that you, with your inversions of faith and doubt, where your faith is in your head and your doubt is in your belly,

that you misused your sword,

by having faith in your perceptions as being solid and real.

By doubting the attachment, the relating, the intimacy, with others.

There is the proper use of doubt, not the doubting of my worth, but doubt in the form of sensing my perceptions

as being nothing more than derived of my other perceptions.

We emerge by deploying faith and doubt not strategically,

but judiciously; not as a way of being in the world, but as a tool.

To be left behind, like leaving the sword on one's way to the baths, or laying aside a hammer to properly open a can of beans.

I hope for you, dear friend, that your practice will become you, that you will leave your fortress.

That i will see you again,

in whatever form you choose.

Chapter 27: Nǐ hǎo

Christine Bennett

Romanticism is intimate, not really sexual. Self discovery, societal revolution and things getting better in general. Think of everything that makes getting laid or falling in love easier, and there's your definition of romanticism.
William Blake is a damn fine example of the romantic revolution. This reads like Duncan [LaPlante] *wrote it.*

—From an email from Miles to Christine, in which he discussed what he'd been reading on the subject of Romanticism in early history.

From: Miles Holden
Date: July 30, 2007
To: Christine Bennett

Subject: Howdy

I've probably missed my shot at hanging out with you before you go to the big 'n' dry state but I've tried more than once on that land line number you gave me. Whoever always ties it up really talks like an old lady, that is, talks forever.

I'm sure I'll get a shot at seeing you again, likely at such a distant time and place that I couldn't guess where or when at this point, but it should happen. People that were once connected will remain connected; the world likes fucking with people like that.

I wish you all the best out there, and tell your fella the same. Have fun in China, too. By the way, when it says "no photography" over there, it means no photography. Don't fuck with the commies, otherwise you might be the new face on Tiananmen Square. That would be kinda cool, though ... provided that you don't get run down by tanks. And I'll still do research for you so long as I have none of my own, that is if you go back to school down there.

Holden

On 4/5/08, Christine Bennett wrote:

Hey Miles!

Haven't heard from ya in a while.

Talked to Buffy the other day, said you were in a car

accident, are you all right? I didn't even know you were driving now.

On 4/15/08, Miles Holden wrote:

I am definitely headed towards Boston. I have no idea what I want to do with my life but at least I love martial arts. I figure I'll just blindly follow that until I get a better idea.

There's a lot of back-story with the accident thing ... and it turns out I front-flipped the thing [car] and almost got my head smashed in by a two hundred pound, flying steel brick. I can't remember anything from the accident.

At first, I had a faint body memory, but now nothing. Anyway, gotta jet, chickie. Will keep blathering as soon as I have the time.

From: Miles Holden
Date: May 27, 2008
To: Christine Bennett
Subject: Re: better late than never

Different car [now]. It really adds to the confusion. I've got the CD player and sound system I always wanted, good on gas and fast as all hell. All I had to do was do something horrible to my family and break the law?

Keeps me guessing as far as good or bad goes, which I know is good.

One thought that hounds me is that I do know better and had it in my power to stop it a year in advance, six months and two minutes before it happened.

It's scary but I think the only way to make sure you don't make things worse is to do something really big to make it better.

I'm having big thoughts lately, and I don't know if my skull is big enough to hold them.

On 5/11/08, Christine Bennett wrote:

I know I totally spaced out on the birthday thing but I figured a month late wasn't too bad … anyway, I hope you had a good one, I guess you're like 20 now right? Or maybe 19. I heard Buffs sent you a lava lamp. She thought it very fitting.

On 5/12/08, Miles Holden wrote:

I'm twenty now, getting to be an antique. The lava lamp is definitely perfect and I wouldn't be at all surprised if Buffy spent a few months zoning out into it. Be careful for the new Red Menace; wouldn't want to see you in a gulag (political prison spelled wrong).

On 5/15/08, Christine Bennett wrote:

Miles,

What's the method to learn reading an Asian language? As far as I remember you mastered Kanji pretty well and I'm just wondering if there's a trick I should know because I'm getting tired of drawing characters on flashcards and still forgetting them in the morning.

Miles Holden wrote:

As for your Kanji thing, flashcards do suck. This sucks, too, but it works all the way. Write it over and over again, try to do about five at a time according to some system. They sink in really fast when your hand does it. I'll check this more often now. Sorry to leave you at the mercy of flashcards.

Chapter 28: Memories From Tinicum

Miles and I both attended Tinicum Art and Science, a private high school in Ottsville, Pennsylvania. When I first came to Tinicum, it had already been through many changes, and was a small school consisting of a handful of students. The philosophy was based on Zen Buddhism—complete with a meditation in the morning—and classes were very small, sometimes only consisting of one or two students. I can recall college level courses I enjoyed, such as Abnormal Psychology and a class devoted to Shakespeare. While I took yoga class for my gym credit, Miles thrived in the Dojo where he learned Shim Gum Do from John Heinz, our headmaster whom he greatly admired.

Tinicum was a family, and though I graduated in 2005, I continue to keep in touch with teachers and former students. Miles found the support he'd always needed at Tinicum Art and Science. Here, teachers and fellow students share their memories.

Matthew Kustafik – Instructor – poetry teacher, and friend

Being a teacher at the high school that Miles graduated from, I was able to see him navigate his tumultuous teen years (not without some difficulty) and carve his own unique path in the world after TAS. He visited the school often, long after he graduated. As I write this my heart grows heavy again, as it does every time since he has passed, remembering that he will never walk through the doors of the school he loved so much, that he found refuge and safety in. His spirit, however, will live with me and the school forever. Miles was a very unique, genuine, caring, intelligent, and funny person. He had a sardonic sense of humor, and a great laugh that I will always remember and miss hearing.

Miles was fortunate to have an older sister, Rosa, who also graduated from TAS. She too is a beloved member of the TAS community and the reason you are reading this now. Thank you, Rosa, for this tribute to your little brother you loved so much. He couldn't have asked for a better sister.

He will be forever loved and fondly remembered.

Buffy Parvin – Instructor – Chef, yoga teacher, and friend

Miles was always sweet, respectful, and kind to me. He'd always stop by the kitchen to say hello, give a hug, and have a nice chat. Once in a while we'd have a deeper discussion usually about some pretty far outer dimensional phenomena. I knew we connected when I shared my fondness for Dr. Who with him and he brought in all these videos he recorded to show me. When I did try to view them, the quality was so poor they were indistinguishable ... it was his gesture of enthusiasm that grabbed me more than any episode ever could have. In passing the dojo he'd often be in there working his forms completely immersed as everyone passed by. It was unusual to see a student by himself in the dojo working out, but not uncommon to see him there ... perhaps this was the place he felt most confident or most secure. Like some lava in a lamp.

Julia Altabef – Student – Friend

Here's some advice Miles texted to me:

"Take my advice: hug as many people as you can, talk with even more. Talk positive or negative but never mix."

Also, "Big things always come from a lot of little people."

Crystal Ungaretta – Student – Friend

Miles had this way of communicating things without blatantly stating them. He was so clever with his delivery of speech. I can hear him singing "Stuck In the Middle With You." He had this period when he was obsessed with Quentin Tarantino movies. That song was in Reservoir Dogs. I remember him doing little jigs to Dropkick Murphy songs as he sung along, or rapping to ICP.

Chapter 29: The Gift

Laura Kemmerer

The first time I met Miles, he was laughing.

At the time, I was still new to Tinicum Art and Science, and I had only gotten to know a few people. Even in a school full of wildly different kids, there was something about Miles that made him stand out. Whether it was the fact that he would train in the dojo during lunch or his sense of humor, it's hard to say exactly what initially drew me to him as a person. Whatever it was, getting to know him was one of the greatest gifts I've ever been given.

What Tinicum Art and Science provided was invaluable; it was a place where teenagers were spoken to as adults, encouraged to pursue creative and intellectual pursuits, and where we could express ourselves with the guidance of mentors who cared deeply about our safety and wellbeing.

Meeting and getting to know Miles within that framework was something that fundamentally changed my perspective on things. As a teenager, I took myself very seriously. He was the first person to teach me how to laugh at myself. He was in my graduating class to boot. Those formative years spent around him—and the other TAS kids—laid the foundation for who I am today.

As our friendship continued past high school, Miles rapidly became the friend that surfaced at unexpected times, and disappeared just as quickly. But it was his way, I think. When I got to hang out with him, it was like no time had passed at all. Miles was always Miles. We could pick up right where we left off.

Miles was one of the only people I could speak to in my early twenties about what I was truly passionate about. He had this talent for speaking to people "where they were"—speaking to their own perspective while being able to teach them and expand their horizons. Any time I heard him speak to someone, even if he was joking around, I never heard him mock someone for not understanding something. In this way, he also taught me to truly listen. I have dreams of eventually becoming a professor, which I now know were directly inspired by him and his treatment of others.

Miles also said a lot of really strange things sometimes. It was almost like he was five minutes ahead of the conversation, and everyone else was still catching up. As our mutual friend, Justin Kreisher, said at his memorial, "Miles would say things that didn't make sense at the time, but weeks later they started to become clear." Miles's influence on my own life has had a similar result—his friendship and wisdom and kindness helped things become clear, especially in the murk of my teenage years and early twenties. His gifts were given before they were needed.

He was, and is, one of the most intelligent men I have ever known. There are times where I still reach for my phone to text him if I've seen something I thought he'd like, or I was just thinking of him. There are other times where I sit in the silence of the night and a bottomless pit feels like its swallowed my stomach. He should still be here, is the mantra that runs through my head.

But we must appreciate the gifts we are given, no matter their longevity or time of arrival. It was a blessing to have known him, and I only hope I can give the gifts he has given me to others.

I miss you. We all miss you.

Chapter 30: Expect The Unexpected

Josh Mertz

I loved Miles. He was like a brother to me.

I started going to Tinicum and was always depressed and had no drive to do anything. I hated my life. I was then introduced to Miles by Stephanie. And from there, I felt I had something to do and have someone to talk to. It was amazing. Miles would take time out of his life to come to the school just to help me. He is my role model and idol! Always will be.

I felt we grew so close until I graduated. I live two hours away and just never had time. He was an amazing guy who made me who I am today, and he is a big reason why I'm still here. Miles is truly my hero.

He helped me tremendously, both physically and mentally. When we met, I was big but really beefy. I was on medicine that made me gain weight and doing Kung Fu helped me stay fit. Mentally, I was very unstable and I strongly believe he helped me stay here in this world.

I had nothing, no one, and no interest in anything until I met Miles. We met at least three days a week. I had two free class periods and spent them training with him. He started teaching me Wing Chun Kung Fu. And from time to time, he would teach me combat training and how to fight with and against weapons for self-defense.

I learned a lot from him but the biggest was the martial art. The moves of Wing Chun are very harmful and could hurt anyone. He taught me Wing Chun so I could protect myself.

"You have to fear the unknown," he said to me.

I also remember him saying, "Expect anything coming."

That was the big reason he would teach me, so I could prepare myself, because I was unaware and oblivious to what was happening around me.

When I got into Wing Chun, I decided to focus my high school senior project on what I had been learning. That led me to create the Wing Chun personal interview that can be found in Part 3. Why not write and study what I was already learning?

I had big plans to stick to it and had hopes to open a school in the future, but my graduation from Tinicum, and living so far away, has put a stop to those plans. I never had enough time to come back to see Miles and continue learning. And after a while, my personal life became hectic, and I lost even more time to try to see him.

One thing I will never forget is that Miles always said, "*Semper vigilo.*"

This means *always vigilant*.

Chapter 31: Be Prepared

Julie Renner

Every day was a new adventure with Miles. The cardinal rule was to always be prepared and to start the day out with stretching. Have the necessary tools for what was planned, but keep the load light. He was basic, never had more than he needed of anything.

He was always eager to teach especially when it came to self-defense. He taught me to make sure that I was always aware of my surroundings. You never knew when a threat could occur. He taught me to make sure I was always prepared for it or had an escape route planned.

He encouraged me with my photography, said I was a wayward photographer, which I have since used to describe my photography.

Hiking was a must on a weekly basis. Everywhere we went would become a very Zen adventure, and we talked the whole hike, then soaked in the silence and beauty of where we were once we reached our destination.

The weather didn't matter, and sometimes we just sat under the porch roof, but Miles always had to go outside. I miss those days—intellectual conversation about the littlest things and his coffee and my tea.

Once, we made his whole work vacation into a random trip. He didn't know where we were going, so he wasn't totally pleased, but he trusted me. He carried his knapsack full of everything he could have possibly needed, and was pleased to be the passenger.

His love for outdoors and my love for astronomy mixed well, and I remember seeing the Milky Way and hiking all over Pennsylvania. He had a goal to hike the whole Appalachian Trail, since I started him on bits and pieces. It was exploring the unknown that brought out a certain twinkle in his eyes that wasn't always there.

Meanwhile, he drilled me all the time on self-defense and awareness. Every day when he woke up, training was his routine, followed by coffee. His life was centered on being the best he could be. There was always an open door for him to follow through, to become one step ahead of where he was in that moment. His rules and life lessons from studying martial arts was what he lived every day, every step of the way. From the moment he woke, to the moment he fell asleep.

He was so simple when it came to the world around him, and he wasn't exposed to "normal" elements growing up, so he taught me about the arts and I taught him about everything else. It was an even trade, a crazy adventure, and highly missed now that time has gone by.

Miles was the type of person that once you got to know him, you never forgot him, and he had an everlasting impression on everyone.

He told me, "Never do anything you'll regret. Think about everything first, never act fast."

Sort through the pros, cons, and always be certain. He claimed acting fast would lead to a dangerous situation. He was a wise teacher, and he needed to share his knowledge to help whomever he was around. No matter what it was, he always had something to say, or an impression to make.

Chapter 32: The Helpmate

April Lewis

Miles was a fully certified EMT as well as a martial artist. I was blessed that I got to know him. He was not only my fiancé, my love, and my soul mate, but he was also my best friend. He knew me and the details of my life, my struggles, and my dreams. We were each other's helpers in so many ways. What Miles did for me, no one had ever done for me before.

As of this writing, I am twenty-eight years old, and during my four-year relationship with Miles, I was diagnosed with several health conditions on top of already existing conditions. Due to having so many health problems, as well as trauma in my past, I experienced unexpected symptoms. Miles stuck by my side without any question or complaint. He not only accepted all of me, but he took care of me more times than I can count.

Throughout and after his EMT training, he used what he had learned to help me. Every day he would take my blood pressure and document any changes in my symptoms. One day, I had a total body shut down—one of the worst.

Miles wasn't particularly a big man, and I am not a tiny woman. My apartment is on the second floor, and the stairs are steep. When Miles and I were on our way home one day, I felt myself begin to shut down. We knew we needed to get home quick. I had begun to lose the ability to talk, and I knew I wouldn't be able to stand, sit up, or even hold up my head. I call it a body shut down because that is exactly what it looks like.

Miles pulled the car into the parking lot at my building. At this point, I had started drooling and was unable to sit up. It took all my strength to attempt to fight the shut down. It also took all of Miles's strength to get me into the house. He managed to get me out of the car.

I believe his ability to balance his weight with mine had been learned through his training in Wing Chun as well as his training in as an EMT. More than anything, Miles was a natural when it came to caring for others. Helping people was at the core of his heart, a desire that continually burned within him.

It took us a bit of time to get from the car to the steps.

Then he had to get me up the stairs. Essentially, he carried me while pushing me up the steps at the same time, allowing most of my weight to fall onto him but using what little strength I had to pull on the railings as he pushed. The situation even made us laugh, because it seemed so ridiculous.

Eventually, he got me into the house, and by then I was pretty much unable to move any of my limbs on my own. It took him some time to get me fully into bed, and then he crawled into bed with me. Miles helped me drink water, because I was having difficulty swallowing, and fed me when I was able to eat. He stayed with me and we watched Netflix together.

The body shut down lasted hours, but Miles knew exactly what to do and did it all with a loving smile of his face. There were many times he helped me in this manner. During flare-ups of my other health issues, he never once complained. Instead, he embraced it. He never made me feel like I was annoying him or in the way, never downplayed my pain—he just went with it. Living with chronic health issues can feel lonely. Miles showed me unconditional love through it all. He was more understanding than I could ever expect anyone to be.

Miles helped me in more ways than just taking care of me with my health issues. He was there for me through everything emotional as well. I lost a few friends in those four years and also encountered unexpected traumas. He held me many times, wiped away my tears, listened to my thoughts, and comforted me.

Miles was good at taking care of me because he knew pain, and he knew it well.

It wasn't until our last year and half together that I was able to return that comfort to him as he began to open up. Miles and I shared the intensity of the two most overwhelming feelings I can imagine, both separately and together: we both knew pain, and we both knew the feeling of being in love.

Chapter 33: My Cousin

Carlos Holden-Villars

I must be honest. I never really knew Miles that well. I saw him on average once every summer, maybe less. We would always exchange pleasantries and ask the same formal questions about our lives. My first memory of Miles is him swimming in the creek in front of Gramma's house, and the most recent one is when he visited our house a few months before he passed away. But I do have one clear, vivid memory of my cousin.

It was early September 2011, a few days before I would start high school. Dad and I went up to Gramma's house to help her move out, and Miles came to help. He was dressed in his usual attire—baggy jeans and a colorful t-shirt. I can still picture the scene—dust, sweat, interesting random objects we found, including some provocative pre-war postcards. We had quite a lengthy conversation about those. I worked with Miles during the entire day, and there was plenty of candid talk between us.

That was the first day I really got to know Miles and experience his enthusiasm and inquisitiveness. There was something that I immediately noticed—his fascination with everything. Miles had a remarkable ability to perceive everything in his own idiosyncratic way. He was constantly asking thought provoking questions, and he was always eager to engage in deep conversations. In fact, it took much longer to clear out the shed mainly because we ended up having discussions about every random object that we found.

At the end of the day, I decided to go for a walk around Gramma's property. I was in a bit of a philosophical mood, musing about things I had never thought of before. Then I realized Miles's inquisitiveness had rubbed off on me. That is perhaps what I appreciate most about Miles—his infectious desire to know more, to question. I regret the fact that there weren't as many opportunities for engrossing talks with him. But at least I was lucky enough to experience his unique personality. And for that, I can't thank him enough.

Chapter 34: The Godshall Family

Fifteen years passed before Miles and I got to see our father again. In 2008, we reunited with him, Dennis Godshall Sr., as well as the rest of the Godshalls. We couldn't have known we would only have three years to get to know our father again before he was rendered comatose, and eventually died due to a four-wheeler accident at age fifty-seven. Here, family share their sorrow in the wake of losing both Dennis and Miles— four years apart—yet, we know they are together once again.

Miles's other sisters, Ashley, Alyssa, and Nicole did not have enough time to get to know him as well as they should have. However, the loss still hit hard, and perhaps it was the loss of "what might have been" that proved most painful.

Donna Godshall Hayden – Aunt

Miles and Rosa came back into our lives after not seeing them since they were small children. I'm angry because they only got to know their father, my brother Dennis, for a few short years as young adults before Dennis died and then we only had a few years before Miles joined his father.

I didn't get enough time to really know Miles. Like his father, he withheld himself from people. I'm angry that we weren't given that time. I just wish him peace and the final knowledge of how much everyone loved him.

Alyssa Godshall – Sister

Even though I didn't know Miles that well, he was still always in my heart. He changed my view of people and how wise people can be, just by having small conversations with him.

Ashley Godshall – Sister

Miles was an amazing man. Although he wasn't involved in my life very much, he still had an impact on me. He changed a lot about me. I was weak before he passed. I didn't feel like I had much. But you don't know how important someone is until they are gone, right? I still love Miles. I wear a bandana around my knee as a symbol. You better believe I'm gonna keep it.

Nicole M. Castillo – Sister

My brother, my brother

    I find myself thinking of you often

Picturing your face

Wondering where you are and if you're watching us

Your passing deeply saddened us. No one was ready to let you go.

Tears well up in my eyes when I think back to the day we found out.

At the same time, I'm comforted by the fact that you're no longer in pain

No sadness, no heartbreak, or confusion

And that unique, beautiful soul of yours will forever shine through our memory and live in our hearts.

I will continue to traipse through this life, keeping you in my mind, hoping I'm making you proud.

My brother, my brother, I love you.

Now and forever. I'll see you again, someday.

Chapter 35: Still Chillin'

Joëlle Rublee

I wanted to walk to Wawa with Miles—the nearest convenience store—in my bare feet, but I didn't call out my true desires, I just watched him leave. That was a Sunday, and the following Sunday I would find out what I had thought, that he was dead.

I don't remember our first encounter. I was at a new school that was like nothing I had known before. We had smoke breaks! This was probably where we stared awkwardly at each other with mutual attraction, our high school hormones raging. He with a rolled cigarette that continuously needed lighting, myself with a pack of Marlboro Lights that I had stolen from my parents.

He asked me, "How goes it?" with the lighted tobacco hanging from his mouth.

Over the years, he has asked me that same question over

and over, which I cannot help but answer with total honesty. The way he would ask, it would never suffice to hand him an account of your average feelings, because he wanted and encouraged honesty.

I find myself stuck in certain places just thinking of Miles. I will be on my way home and the thoughts begin. Then I just continue driving and driving, with the music turned up. No matter what song it is, I don't listen. It is just the sound of his words or the memory of his actions that play through my mind. I try to fit the pieces together but it never satisfies me.

When I received his last call, I had just been to 7-11, and his voice on my speaker phone resounded of fright and need. I didn't let go 'til the line ended.

Every Friday in high school, we had a cleaning. On most of these weeks, Miles and I were assigned to the dojo, a coincidence or some clever maneuverings from a boy with a crush.

I remember Miles saying, "You are the only person that I trust with cleaning the dojo."

He always held such a respect for this room and practice. The term mindfulness was constantly being thrown around, but for us, it was a way of living. Even the thought of losing your mug in between classes was something that both of us remained cognizant of. He understood me in a way that no one else ever acknowledged—an understanding and appreciation of my spirituality without ever having to give a definition.

After the fourth time I tried calling back on that night, I figured his phone had finally broken for good, something he had made a point of telling me. He had thrown his phone across the room after he saw a woman get punched by her boyfriend outside his window. This act shook him, it wasn't a purposeful hit to the woman, rather she had gotten in the way of another man in the dispute. Seeing the woman fall to the ground disrupted his mission, the need for teaching others self-defense; it isn't only self-defense that is needed, but a desire for putting others first. The battle between being selfish and selfless is something even a bible and an all powerful being cannot solve.

Pennsylvania summers have always been so romantic in my eyes. It is almost like living in a southern state without the racist overtones. We have the beautiful plants, the humid days, and the raging thunderstorms. The summer that Miles and I were together were filled with all of those. I would drive to his house in the afternoon and we would spend the evening exploring the area around his house, smoke out of tool parts, and spar 'til it led to a make-out session. We would also argue about everything, and I would say my car was light and he would insist it was heavier than eighteen steers on their way to the slaughterhouse. His side always had a certain hyperbole-esque point that could not be contested because of the sheer ridiculousness of it. Though his views calmed down over the years, his arguments continued in this spirit.

One of our last conversations began with a text: "Are there really people that still believe that the earth is flat?"

A friend of mine had told me a story of his significant other that was part of this movement. Of course, I had to ask Miles. He usually had an answer and explanation for everything. He responded in the affirmative and after a few texts back and forth, we were talking on the phone about it.

I was housesitting and I remember walking all around this huge house and pool area, laughing and talking with him about the ridiculousness of it all. As he had studied the bible and many other works of religion, his answers were forthright and thoughtful. His relationship with religion confounded me when I heard of his conversion to Christianity. But I understood later that he was looking for answers that can't be discerned without a larger existence playing a role. It was never blind faith that he followed, it was study and an appreciation of texts that allowed him to believe, but it was also this that led him away from it. It is easier to believe without question; Miles was always questioning.

After a summer of young love, I went away on a backpacking trip. I thought of Miles often but it was always confusing. I am afraid of love, the consequences and the positives. I had a panic attack before a climb on a mountain, which now seems such an easy metaphor. I'm afraid to take it to the limit, with love and myself.

It was the first day back at school and it was just Miles and I outside. He asked, "So are we still chillin'?"

I shook my head no. I couldn't handle that loving look in his eyes. I couldn't handle opening up to someone. He took me as I was which scared the hell out of me. He remains the only person that I could completely open up to, with only love in his eyes and mind. I really wish I had been brave enough to say yes.

My most recent love has become cheese, which seems odd because unless a person is lactose intolerant, all people love cheese. Mine is more the knowledge and the differences in cheeses from around the world. I was able to share this love of cheese with Miles and he loved to hear the different stories behind each new cheese I was learning about.

I must admit that I meant to share many more cheeses than I had with him. When we would talk on the phone, much of it was doom and gloom, both of us dealing with issues of the mind and heart but a way to get out of it was to hear stories of different cheeses. The beginning of cheese: a man that happened to eat the inside of a stomach of a dead baby with their mother's milk inside. Oh, the conversation that came of that! It was a way that I learned to help calm Miles down and he acknowledged that and asked for cheese stories.

The last story I ever told him was that of the cheese Bastardo. It is a mix between mostly cow's milk but with some goat or sheep milk that happen to be part of the herd during the summer. In a way of not wasting any milk, they just add it all together. I meant this story to be fun and light but as a response all I heard was a muffled pop.

After I said, "No," Miles did not look at me for a long time. I knew I had broken his heart but mine was broken, too. I moved to the other coast and began my studies. I never wanted to be stationary and the idea of love seemed like a straitjacket to me. While other college freshmen were coupling up, I held my distance.

I came back home after a time to be present for some kind of Tinicum gathering and Miles was there. We sat outside on the side of the school and started talking like nothing had hurt us both. Lying in the grass, talking about anything, seemed like the most natural thing to do with him or anybody. I went back to the west coast and we would periodically talk for hours about everything and nothing. The time difference was never a factor; if I needed advice, I would call him and he would let me spew. Then he would spew. Our love never faltered, it was just displaced.

After silence for a few moments, I told him I would call him back. I did, five times. No response. I hoped his phone was just destroyed and I had to wake up early the next morning to milk the goats. When I woke up, I tried calling him again. Nothing. And again. Nothing. But who can get a new cell phone at seven in the morning?

I had told him that I would come over at five to see how he was doing but since I didn't hear from him, I didn't take the trip and was waiting for him to show up on Friday like he promised with a dead cell phone and no money to pay for a new one.

I got a call while I was at work on Friday from his contact with the Marines, saying that he hadn't heard from him and wondered if I had. His evaluation was scheduled for Sunday. I assured the officer that his phone was broken and that he would be there but the worry set in. Miles is nothing but on top of his shit. Even my coworkers noticed my distress. As I was trying to talk the Marine into believing nothing had happened, I was also trying to make myself believe.

The longest we hadn't talked since we started again was maybe twelve hours. I wanted to rush from work to his place but I had responsibilities of watching a dog. It seems so trivial now. I called Duncan, one of Miles's favorite people, to see if he had heard from him.

I remember saying, "Maybe I'm not passionate enough," thinking maybe Miles and I had gotten into an argument that he didn't want to talk to me about. Now those words mean to me that I wish I had told him I loved him. Every time we were together, the love from me to him grew stronger but that fear of love and truth still held me back from speaking it. I asked him once why he was hanging out with me again and he replied that when I held him, he felt safe.

Phone calls ... there are only some that actually mean anything. Replying to a debt collector seems like a hard task but it is nothing compared to something that is priceless. Telling Rosa, Miles's big sister, that her brother was no longer in this world was the hardest thing that I have ever had to do.

We both already knew, but to put it into words was something else.

If only I had said yes when he asked if we were still chilling, if only I had replied I felt safe with him too, if only I had told him I loved him. Those *ifs* mean nothing. He struggled and tried. In the end, he chose. His ripples are felt for miles and he broke my heart harder in the end.

Miles's Recommended Reading List

"Application Against Multiple Opponents" and the "Multiple Attackers and Multiple Units" section are both greatly inspired by the material in *The Art of War* by Sun Tzu. By comparison, it's a little vague but it still serves its purpose for urban conflict. It doesn't get too deep into terrain or classic battle movements, and is ideal against three to eight people—hopefully not eight.

Other than that, the major influence for these sections was *FM 3-25 .150* or the *Combatives Manual for the U.S. Army*. It is the basis of the "Unarmed Combat" section.

The works of Ashida Kim have played a huge role in nearly every section—hunting, knife fighting, foreign weapons, empty hand to a certain extent, and targeting in general.

The book used primarily for these sections was *Secrets of the Ninja*, a book that covers insertion and extraction, termination and stealth. Still, it wasn't the primary source for any of these concepts or sections.

FM 7-85, Ranger Unit Operations, played an enormous part in the fine details and general structure of stealth evasion and combat. The Ranger is one of the best modern expressions of anything remotely close to Ninjistsu, except that we have outdone it since its introduction into military training methods.

The unarmed section was fueled by FM 3-25 .150, the Combatives Manual for the Military. It is an excellent source for grappling, boxing, and some weapons technique.

I chose this manual because of these simple words in the beginning: "The fundamental truth of hand-to-hand fighting is that the winner will be the one whose buddies show up first with a weapon. Given modern equipment, complicated scenarios, and the split seconds available to make life and death decisions, soldiers must be armed with practical and workable solutions." Make that the core of your training.

Newsletter No. 1-88 and 2-88. These are historical in nature. The errors and victories in half-baked strategy must be exposed for a successful offensive or defensive movement in the future. It's not so applicable to defending the self or even fighting in teams, but knowing all you can is at the core of any pursuit.

Championship Fighting, Explosive Punching and Aggressive Defense is one of the most informative books on boxing, written by one of the most revolutionary fighters, Jack Dempsey. This did not begin as a reference. It still doesn't qualify, because if it was, the boxing section would be about ten pages longer, and a lot more in-depth. Certain details that should have been included, I gleaned from this book and it was too late to throw it in by then.

Other Books and Publications Miles Enjoyed

The Encyclopedia of the Sword by Nick Evangelista, foreword by William M. Gaugler. Greenwood Press.

Hagakure: The Book of the Samurai by Yamamoto Tsunetomo and William Scott Wilson (translator). Shambhala Publications.

Hávamál, presented as a single poem in the *Codex Regius*, a collection of Old Norse poems from the Viking age.

Mind Over Matter: Higher Martial Arts by Shi Ming with Siao Weijia (translated by Thomas Cleary)

The Wing Chun Compendium, Volume 1 by Wayne Belonoha. Blue Snake Books.

Glossary

C.C.B., Common Carry Blade – Without hand guards, a blade under four inches. Easy to conceal.

Centerline – The *centerline* is the imaginary line running from between the eyes to the genitals and occasionally a leg. Your most sensitive targets are here, excluding the temples, eardrums, and mastoid process.

Close Quarter Termination – This involves the combinations and footwork version of the boxing section. Primarily, it's thought-based instead of based in repetitive training.

Compulsive Cover – Compulsive cover is the concept of compulsively or instinctively guarding the face, throat, and solar plexus.

First Strike Strategy – Always have a plan and be prepared for anything. First strike strategy involves being able to go from relaxed to tense in less than a second when threatened.

MADE (Minimize, Act, Disrupt, Execute) – A strategy of self-defense created by Miles Dylan Holden, designed to teach stance, blocking, attacking, objectives, and mindset. Made to enhance the likelihood of survival in a dangerous situation.

Line in the Sand – The minimum measurement of space, one full step away from your sphere of influence. The line in the sand begins where your sphere of influence ends.

Powell Doctrine – An attitude that tactics and tools are filtered through. The philosophy of hitting as hard as you can, as early as you can. Surprise is its primary asset.

Puppet Theory – This theory operates on the idea that a human body is connected by tendons. If you are attacked, a common carry blade can be used to cut tendons in a struggle, like cutting the strings on a puppet. The approach ends the attack without killing the attacker, giving you time to call for help.

S.A.S.C (Structural, Airway, Sensory, and Circulation) – Framework for knife application. During an attack, damaging one of these factors throws off the balance of your attacker. S.A.S.C. should be used with the overall intent to destroy your opponent's balance.

Snapping Technique – This technique keeps the opponent from being able to manipulate your punch because it is so quick. The theory behind snapping technique is that it gives the opponent little opportunity to retreat.

Sphere of Influence – The exact range you can control without moving. In terms of the unarmed combatant: it is the length of your arm. In terms of the armed combatant: it is the length of your weapon.

Standard Response – Take ground, thrust, hit, thrust until your opponent is grounded. This is economy of motion at its best. The advanced application of the standard response should include a throw, reap, or severe damage to the knee.

Two hands, one leg / inside entry – The name of the last dummy form in the Moy Yat Wing Chun lineage.

Waster – A wooden training sword.

Index

B

Balance, 44, 148, 173
Books, 177, 265
Boxing, 30, 60, 187

C

Colin Powell, 51, 187, 268
Combat Technique, 52, 58, 60, 61, 63, 65, 66, 70, 71, 73, 74, 75, 79, 80, 89, 110, 120, 123, 125, 126, 127, 128, 133, 137, 138, 145, 147, 148, 171, 172, 181, 182, 183, 263, 264, 268, 269

E

EMT, 145, 169, 244, 245
Environment, 89, 95

F

Famous Martial Artists, 111, 155
Forms, 158, 162, 166, 167, 171, 175, 176, 178, 179, 187

H

History, 227
Human Body, 83

K

Karate, 30, 115
Knife Technique, 99, 101, 103, 106, 120, 123, 138, 140, 142, 145, 149

M

MADE, 23, 25, 35, 36, 38, 42, 45, 46, 111, 172, 268
Martial Arts Systems, 187

Movies, 169

N

Neighborhood Rules, 23, 58, 92, 120, 123

S

Safety, 144, 166

Shim Gum Do, 157, 174, 179, 185, 187, 232, 241

Single Opponent, 92

Stick Fighting, 58

Structural, Airway, Sensory, Circulation, 146, 162, 163, 166, 269

Systems, 30, 116, 141

T

Targeting System, 58, 65, 66, 120, 128, 268

Teachers, 9, 44, 56, 161, 232

Tinicum Art and Science, 9, 23, 193, 194, 203, 232, 235

Tools, 77, 118

Training, 87, 88, 95, 138, 175

W

Weaponry, 57, 109, 110, 131, 141, 142, 160

Wing Chun, 10, 39, 56, 59, 60, 61, 70, 98, 126, 142, 147, 150, 155, 158, 160, 161, 171, 172, 177, 181, 267, 269

Wrestling, 30

Writers, 161, 227

About M. D. Holden

M. D. Holden (Miles Dylan Godshall Holden) was born in Old Zionsville, Pennsylvania. He is the author of numerous articles on self-defense and Wing Chun, a form of Chinese self-defense. This book is a compilation of his writings.

Miles experimented with techniques and studied Wing Chun and martial arts for ten years, and became an instructor himself. He also studied Shim Gum Do and received his high school diploma from Tinicum Art and Science, a Zen-based private school in Ottsville, Pennsylvania which focused on mindfulness in all things. He was a certified EMT, driven to help those around him.

In August of 2015, Miles took his own life at age 27. However, he has left behind a brief legacy of love, kindness, caring, and humor which is clearly present in his writing. Miles's unique personality and his own "sphere of influence" on those around him will never be forgotten.

Search "M. D. Holden" on Facebook and like Miles's Fan Page (managed by Lady June Press).

About Rosa Sophia

Rosa Sophia is the author of *Meet Me in the Garden* (Limitless Publishing), *Over the Ivy Wall* (Sunshine Press) and others. She is an editorial consultant and freelance writer, currently residing in South Florida in a cottage by the sea. Visit her website, the Backwords Writer: www.backwordswriter.com

www.ingramcontent.com/pod-product-compliance
Lightning Source LLC
Chambersburg PA
CBHW020924090426
42736CB00010B/1025